Mary-Ann
A pleasure to work with you
and a thousand thanks for your
skilled editing and your generosity.
David
January. 2007

BATTLEFIELD WITHOUT BORDERS

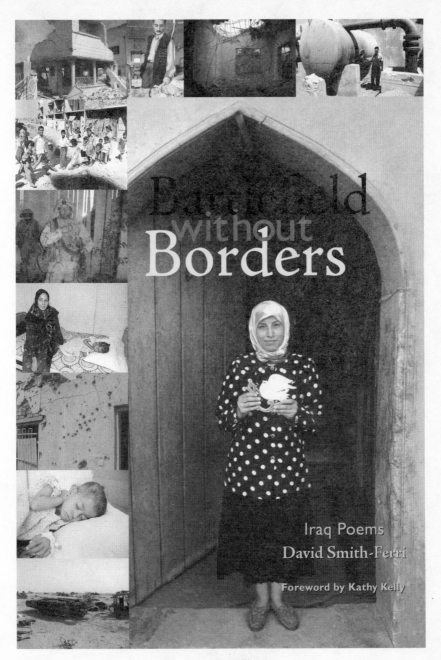

Battlefield without Borders

Iraq Poems

David Smith-Ferri

Foreword by Kathy Kelly

Haley's
Athol, Massachusetts

Haley's
Post Office Box 248
Athol, Massachusetts 01331
1.800.215.8805 • haley.antique@verizon.net
www.haleysantiques.com
Printed in China

With thanks to Mary-Ann DeVita Palmieri.

The frontispiece photograph of Umm Heyder and her son Mustafa in their Basra home was taken by David Smith-Ferri in 2002.

Smith-Ferri, David, 1960-
  Battlefield without borders / by David Smith-Ferri.
    p. cm.
  Includes bibliographical references.
  ISBN-13: 978-1-884540-80-5
  1. Iraq War, 2003---Poetry. 2. Americans--Iraq--Poetry. 3. Protest poetry, American. I. Title.
  PS3619.M5965B38 2007
  811'.6--dc22

                          2006033815

For Kathy Kelly and Barbara Lubin, showing the way.

And for Rachael, finding her way.

Contents

Illustrations

Kathy Kelly and Sattar Jabbar at the bombed-out Children's Teaching Hospital in Baghdad, December 1998. Kathy is holding a lamp to shed light on the truth.

—Photo by Alan Pogue

A Pen like a Paintbrush, a foreword by Kathy Kelly

In the late 1990s, when economic sanctions brutally and lethally punished innocent Iraqis, Voices in the Wilderness delegations tried to dispel the dangerous notion, so prevalent in the United States, that only one person lived in Iraq, the notorious dictator Saddam Hussein. David Smith-Ferri carried his pen into Iraq like a paintbrush, painting images of ordinary Iraqi people and evoking a consistent, irresistible desire to build friendly and fair relationships. His poems ignite stubborn hope in "person-to-person diplomacy," as ordinary US and UK people nonviolently defied the economic sanctions by bringing medicines to children and families in Iraq.

We were traveling into a police state. The regime was well aware of every step we took. We didn't want to be used as dupes for the regime's propaganda. But the alternative of walking away from the bedsides of dying children, murmuring our apologies to bewildered and grieving mothers, and giving up on any possibility of return was unacceptable. David returned repeatedly, insistently, creating a poet's chronicle of the devastation endured by people who meant us no harm, who longed for release from their punishment.

David's poem, "The Beast in Baghdad," written in September of 2002, begins with these lines:

> We saw the Beast again in Baghdad,
> second time in two days.
> No, not Saddam Hussein, his presidential smile
> only half concealing the armaments behind his eyes,
> but a deadlier menace:
> depleted uranium, cold and unadorned.
> On cots in wards and on chairs in hallways,
> children sat, slowly roasting,
> leukemia a fire in their bones and blood.

Describing Baghdad shortly before the diabolically named shock and awe campaign began, before "an immense wrecking ball of war swung outward on its taut cable," Smith-Ferri depicts :

> A time when an anxious sky held its breath, when sentinel date palms
> stood watching, when all of Baghdad waited.

Nurturing hopes that somehow, perhaps in six months' time, they could begin a journey toward the normalcy they longed to provide for their children, many Iraqis awaited the US arrival. They didn't understand the intent of the shock and awe strategy. The Chicago *Sun Herald* reported,

> The US intends to shatter Iraq physically, emotionally, and psychologically by raining down on its people as many as eight hundred cruise missiles in two days . . . more than twice the number of missiles launched during the entire forty days of the 1991 Gulf War . . . The Pentagon battle plan aims not only to crush Iraqi troops, but also to wipe out power and water supplies in the capital, Baghdad.

Now, three years later, the US occupation of Iraq continues to elevate US interests in markets, material resources, cheap labor, and strategic geopolitical control.

Smith-Ferri continues to wage a battle, crafted through words and images, against the narrow and confining propaganda that declares the war was worth it because, after all, we got rid of Saddam Hussein. In "Global Heart," he beckons us to look into a mirror and there discover the illness of victors:

> Now, Saddam Hussein stands in court,
> the ex-king of a hundred palaces,
> the fox who never slept in the same den two consecutive nights.
> Now that he is reduced to a mere man clinging to a deadly fantasy,
> now that he stands in a bright pool of public scrutiny,
> we see more clearly than ever our own government reflected in that pool
> and drowning in similar messianic delusions,
> addicted to the same violent methods, blood-blind,
> willing to sacrifice without end other people's daughters and
>   sons, fathers and mothers.

If we single out one war criminal and hold just one person responsible for gross violations of human rights, then we will never understand our own complicity. During the agonizing years of the Iran-Iraq war from 1980 to 1988, the United States competed with other governments to sell weapons to Iraq and to assure that Iraq would have the means to purchase those weapons, even the components of chemical weapons. The United States supplied Iraq with satellite photos of Iranian troop movements and also the analysts to interpret those photographs so that the Iraqi troops would know where and when to launch chemical and other weapons against Iranian troops.

When President George Bush Sr. could have unseated the Iraqi regime, following the Desert Storm war, the US government instead allowed Saddam Hussein to keep his attack helicopters, enabling him to use air superiority to squelch uprisings in the north and south of Iraq. Even the sanctions helped maintain Saddam Hussein's regime, crippling Iraq externally, but strengthening the regime internally as Iraqi civilians became increasingly dependent on the government for rations and were almost totally isolated from contacts with the world beyond their borders.

Saddam Hussein stands in a pool of public scrutiny as the court calls forth witnesses to tell of the suffering they endured under his regime. But the court of public opinion cannot bend toward justice without our willingness to look in the mirror and see ourselves as accomplices to the murderous policies that have afflicted Iraqi people since the United States first helped Saddam Hussein establish a dictatorship in Iraq. As Americans, we were more responsible for the regime of Saddam Hussein than was any Iraqi man, woman, or child described in the pages of this book.

I hope the most lasting effect of *Battlefield without Borders* will be a blurring of borders as listeners and readers imagine themselves dwelling in a world no longer dominated by an imperial menace. In "Global Heart," Smith-Ferri writes:

> We long to see the fantasy laid bare, stripped to its lethal, radioactive core
>   and contained,
> a circular fence erected around it, signs declaring *Danger!* and seven guards
>   posted at its gate.
> In our yearning, we join ourselves to people in Iraq, to people everywhere,
> a global heart longing to see State greed and arrogance revealed for
>   what they are:
> a poisonous and bloody sword, polluting the Earth, killing our loved ones.
> This is our common ground.
> Let's build here.

In these poems, David Smith-Ferri's creative intelligence focuses on insidious forces of war, forces that often cause people to shrink in fear. He appeals to our best instincts, urges us to overcome fear, and dares to offer trust and friendship as the basis for creating better social structures. In this sense his poetry is utterly useful and necessary, akin to a brilliant blueprint, beckoning builders.

A crowd gathered after a US missile strike in Najaf, July 20, 1999

-photo by David Smith-Ferri

The Same Four Words

After learning about the massacre in Haditha
May, 2006

The war ended.
Light bulbs flashed at a press conference
and an American president declared, a second time,
    "Mission accomplished."
In a palace in Washington,
ink flowed from pens
and official papers, like a conjurer's voice through cupped hands,
called our soldiers home,
called our weaponry away, away.

In Iraq, in the silence that followed,
in the emptiness,
a shocked landscape exhaled.
In Haditha, a sleeping child in her arms,
a woman sat on a stone wall
under a bleached sky.
Listen to my story, she said.

Nine thousand miles away,
in a Marine barracks near San Diego,
soldiers awaiting trial awoke from nightmares
murmuring the same four words:
Listen to my story.

Across Iraq and in refugee communities in Jordan and Syria,
twenty million people stepped out of their homes.
Listen to my story about the war, they said.
The words that followed were too many to count,
    too hot to hold.
They burned to a fine dust that trade winds lifted
and carried across continents and over oceans
to North America, where it darkened skies over southern California
then fell onto a military courthouse.
Dust drifted across roof tiles and down walls.
Like infinite fingers it probed the building, seeking an opening.
It blew against doors and windows and foundation.
But the hermetic architecture barred its entry.

Across America, in rural towns and in large cities,
in hospitals and bedrooms and grocery stores,
soldiers and the families of soldiers said,
Listen to my story . . .
The words rumbled and thundered,
Listen to my story . . . Listen to my story . . .
They assailed that same courthouse,
but the building stood, impassive and insulated against that sound.

Inside, lawyers and bureaucrats tried the soldiers
and a military judge found them criminal.
They tried the Iraqis *in absentia* and declared them illegal, alien.
The inadmissible dust, like toxic waste, they deported.
But the pestilential war, thriving in its presidential host,
breeding in government bodies,
never entered the room,
never looked the law in the eye.

Every Iraqi Knows

June–July, 2006

Every Iraqi knows
there are lions in the desert.
And by now, every Iraqi knows
the American soldiers stalked Abeer like lions,
in a pack,
the leaders among them taking the first bites
of her fifteen-year-old flesh.

A US official called it
a "crime of opportunity,"
but every Iraqi knows that—
crouching behind lies the size of boulders,
monitoring winds,
moving through a grassy savannah of misinformation,
assured of the entitlement of their sex, their race,
their weaponry—
they stalked her
as Cheney and Rumsfeld stalked Iraq.

They singled Abeer out
as the neocons singled out Iraq,
for its vulnerability,
for the treasures hidden beneath the plain folds of its dress.

They raped her
as the Coalition Provisional Authority raped Iraq,
forcing its legs,
authorizing foreign capital to penetrate, to seed itself.

And after raping her,
after killing her parents and her younger sister,
they poured petrol
and set her on fire.
She burned just as Iraq burns,
blue and orange flames devouring its body,
thick, black smoke scorching the throat and eyes
of anyone who tries to watch,
who tries to scream for help.

Standing There

After the death of Abu Musab al-Zarqawi
June, 2006

Carried on radio waves,
news of Abu Musab al-Zarqawi's death reached me
with unexpected force and in an unlikely place:
a Buddhist monastery.
It is a place where violence, in any form, is forbidden entrance,
and where vast internal spaces are mirrored
by the boundless natural landscape.
Nuns and monks, in simple robes, walk and work.
Radiant peacocks and peahens strut.
Students, aged six to eighteen, study in a school
that emphasizes character
and asks, *How can you be of service to the world?*
Above it all, like guardians, massive oaks and sycamores spread their arms.

The news arrived as I fastened my safety belt,
and suddenly I felt anything but safer.
Two five-hundred-pound bombs, a radio voice said,
enough explosive bite in their jaws to swallow a house
and leave a house-sized crater in a date palm orchard.
Like a meteor, I thought. *Sudden, suicidal, alien.*

Al-Zarqawi, the disembodied voice of terrorist threats,
his actual body, broken and bloody, now a war trophy.

Who doesn't want to see an end to terror in Iraq,
an end to exploding cars and baby carriages,
to looking for missing relatives in morgues?

I stepped out of my car.

Standing there,
I more than half expected those great trees to swoon,
the ground to turn momentarily fluid.

Days before, Rachael had told a story.
It seemed simple then.
A bug flew into my eye while I played soccer.
For a full minute,
I stumbled across the field, half-blind, frantically blinking,
trying to free the bug,
holding my big, clumsy fingers at my side.
It was hilarious.
Teammates told me, "Just kill it,"
but I laughed and blinked,
and the bug broke free.

Standing there alongside the sycamores,
I could not reconcile the two images:
on the one hand, the Fighter Falcon and its ferocious
    bombs finding their target
and on the other the foolish fourteen-year-old, fumbling,
    finding another way.

Standing there outside the Buddhist elementary and secondary schools,
I couldn't help wonder which image would flower,
which image would seed our future:
the grown men in the F-16 following orders to kill
or the girl-woman, following a voice only she can hear.

Battlefield without Borders

after talking to Sattar
May, 2006

Imagine being hunted
and the predator is anyone, anywhere.
Imagine to move is perilous.

Merely to leave our house,
to walk to a neighbor's home or hail and ride a taxi
presses a cold, metal gun barrel against our temple,
spins its chambers, pulls its trigger.
Who can predict an outcome?
Odds, awful odds pursue us.

Our world has resumed its original shape.
Culture has fled. Custom is an empty sack. Nothing is sacred.
Now, even hospitals,
even mosques are ribbed with explosives.
Even people who are sick and those who succor them,
even people who are dead and those who mourn them
    are targets.
There is no sanctuary.
Violence spreads its patterned cloth over our land
    and sets its table.
We eat
and are eaten
daily.

The Dead Are Not Blind

July, 2005

Not only at night,
when five hundred tongues of darkness raise a small fire,
consuming the bedding, walls, and ceiling of my mind
and a thousand bony hands like small bats
awake and beat flaming air,
but every day now I hear them:
voices of the Iraqi dead speaking with the near-dead,
comforting them, cradling their feverish heads and hollow bodies,
accompanying them through the curtain, across dark waters.

And voices of American soldiers and contractors dead in Iraq,
ripped from warm arms of their families,
leaving trails of blood behind them across oceans and deserts,
a red tide, a permanent stain on our land.
They urge their compatriots to lay down their rifles,
to discard their boots and flack jackets,
to step off shore and swim for home.

Pitched at low frequency, these conversations
vibrate through our world.
Distilled, purified, charged with the Earth's electric charge—
like water through earth, enriched with its minerals, aqueous—
they travel below ground.
Springing here, they wash across a sand and gravel bed of my mind,
rearranging it.
Secretive, these conversations travel between buildings,
under floorboards, and through ventilation ducts,
riding hidden currents.
Avian, they sail in pockets of an evening wind,
and seeded in clouds, they rain lightly down.

The dead are not blind,
and I am not the only one who hears voices.

There Are Names

for Barbara Lubin

June, 2006

There are stories we are forbidden to read,
walls behind which we are forbidden to look.

There are places we are forbidden to explore,
holes no light illumines, no stair descends.

There are countries whose names have been erased from maps,
cities whose names are a strangled flame, a quenched fire,
hospitals whose names have been bled dry, sterilized.

Whisper these names and your throat will burn.
Speak them aloud and flames leap from your lips.

Say *Gaza* and *Fallujah.*
Say *Walter Reed Hospital,*
articulating every bloody syllable.
Say *Ramadi*
and see what happens.

These are names you are forbidden to repeat,
forbidden to remember.
These are stories you are forbidden to tell.

The Weapon Is Sanctions

I visited Iraq in 1999 as part of an eight-member fact-finding delega-
tion concerned with the impact of United States foreign policy on Iraq. The
delegation was organized by a group called Voices in the Wilderness. My
purpose was to gather information regarding the effects of the international
economic sanctions and the "no-fly zone" bombings on Iraqi people and
Iraqi society.

A humanitarian crisis had been unfolding in Iraq since the imposition of
sanctions in 1990 though few Americans understood its scope. By destroy-
ing their country's economy, the sanctions thrust Iraqis abruptly into pov-
erty and hopelessness. Malnutrition and child mortality rates soared. Unable
to maintain their sewage treatment facilities and to obtain the chemicals
necessary for water purification, Iraqis watched in horror as deadly bacterio-
logical diseases spread and hospitals ran out of the antibiotics to treat them.

As a United States citizen, alarmed by my government's unflagging
support of an embargo implicated in the deaths of untold thousands of
Iraqi children, I believed I had a right to travel to Iraq to obtain firsthand
information. While in Iraq, I interviewed a wide range of people, includ-
ing United Nations program directors, doctors, hospital patients and their
parents, teachers, lawyers, Muslim and Christian clerics, businessmen, shop
owners, taxi drivers, waiters, and artists. I also visited the sites of recent
bombings and interviewed civilian survivors as well as Iraqi Red Crescent
Society staff who monitored the effects of the "no-fly zone" patrols. At that
time, United States and British war planes bombed Iraq two to three times
a week on average, often injuring or killing Iraqi civilians.

The following poems tell the story of my encounters during that trip.

Departure

Leaving for Iraq
July 17, 1999

I

We board the plane.
For strength and comfort, embarkations invite comparisons.
Like a beggar his pants, I search
the pockets of my mind, my past.

Come up,
besides dust and lint,
empty handed.

II

The great ship shudders;
every bolt and screw, every seam strains.
The huge bird, wings spread, sprints honking.
The runway liquefies.
Webbed feet slap the water and leap aloft
revealing our fragility.

Our bodies, our mission
for the moment, in the care of Jordanian Air.

III

Silence.
A hush,
not of alert minds and attentive hearts,
of awe before majesty and mystery,
a silence that precedes *alleluia!*
but silence begetting silence, without end,
a totalitarian silence.

The whole land is silent—
women in labor, babies at birth,
birds at dawn, at dusk,
planes departing and landing,
all silent.

Listen.
The plane glides noiselessly over Illinois, Ohio, Pennsylvania . . .
heading for Amman.
Brace yourself. Somewhere soon,
over some sea or land not ours,
it will pierce the barrier,
unleashing a scream like sonic boom:

Sanctions kill!

End of the Conversation

Saddam General Hospital, Baghdad
July 23, 1999

No scratch or scuff on the glazed brow of the sky,
and beneath its spacious skull,
a single, imperious thought burns in that blue, cavernous mind.
Daily, like a sorcerer, the sun warms Iraq's sewage-laden rivers,
conjuring cholera and typhoid and E. coli
that are killing children in this hospital ward,
slowly draining juice from their tiny bodies.
Here lies the desiccated fruit of a generation.

Outside in a depression,
raw sewage backs up against a south compound wall,
a gangrenous green pool twenty feet across,
daring us to cling to a fantasy that hospitals
are immune to environmental contamination.

The head doctor sets us straight.
When we open the tap here,
we get the same flow of polluted water
that brings these patients in the first place.
It's a long shadow; there is no escape.
Even the dead are washed in it.

Space is at a premium.
Along every wall, their mothers sitting next to them,
young children lie on cots
and also at our feet on the cement floor, a thin wrap serving as a bed,
thin as the membrane here between life and death.
The doctor introduces us, diagnoses the child's illness,
and translates as we speak with the mother.

Mary, a member of our group, asks for a prognosis,
and so, like a metronome, at each bed the doctor informs us:
This child will die . . . That child will die . . . This child will die . . .
A grim, tour-weary guide.

Flies swarm, extras in a drama without end.
Rank, humid air weighs on our chests.

Mary persists: *What do you say to the parents?*
When they look to you for hope, what do you say to them?

Shaking his head definitively, the doctor responds:
There is no hope.
They're going to die.
And then slowly, sucking the oxygen out of the room,
They're all going to die.

The Unmistakable Imprint of Love

Saddam General Hospital, Amara
July 25, 1999

In this sad place, powerlessness is a voracious presence,
unappeased and pathologic. It eats flesh,
a bacteria consuming people from within,
emptying everyone who comes here,
leaving patients, their parents, the doctors like hollowed reeds.

Or so we thought.
When the air moved,
we expected a mournful tune.

For three hours this morning,
stopping as planned at each cot,
we walked slowly through the pediatrics wards,
observing children caught in the swollen river of sanctions:
tiny bodies tossed by the tide,
hands groping for a root, a branch,
but torn downriver by the implacable current.
Taking measurements and securing water samples for analysis,
we calculated the depth of the river, its width,
the number of feet above flood stage.

At one bedside, I held Hassan, a featherweight, eight-month-old child.
Dying there slowly, he slept in my arms.
His mother smiled; she spoke to me directly, in Arabic.
Turning for help, I felt on every side
the fixed, expectant eyes of other mothers holding me,
waiting for my response,
even as I waited for her words to come out of hiding.
Doctor Khammas came across the room to translate.

She said, "If you can heal my child, please take him with you."
I struggled to breathe,
and the plain meaning of those words came from too far away,
came so slowly toward me
as though swimming through a great depth of water.
I handed Hassan back to his mother,
who smiled graciously, without the least cruelty,
and the mothers' eyes released me.
But the electrical surge of their desire
marked me forever:
the unmistakable imprint of love.

Letter to Rachael

for my seven-year-old daughter

Amara
July 25, 1999

We pass for pilgrims,
dusty, endangered, hangers on,
and a squint-eyed prick of light in the dark night of our minds
passes for a star.

Thus we enter a malnutrition ward of Amara General Hospital
with no gift to offer that gesture of hand cannot summon
or eye to eye bestow.

In this room: eight beds . . . eight mothers . . .
eight infants, a single mask of starvation.

     * * *

Seekers, we are searched.
Every mother's eye beholds us,
and every child's face, Rachael,
is your face.

In the Tenth Year of Sanctions, A Dinner Party

Baghdad
July, 1999

Like late-stage, terminally ill patients granted a sudden ten-day reprieve of
good health,
we packed the days with people—UN program directors, doctors, clerics,
teachers—
squeezing the juice from every encounter,
meeting late into the night, and sleeping little in the impossible heat.
So when an invitation to a dinner party came,
we accepted as custom required and eyed also a chance for a night off.

Our host: Yusef Habi, an old Chaldean priest and scholar.
A small group gathered, all his friends:
local businessmen, fellow priests, a writer from Paris, an Iraqi painter,
enough Americans to go around exactly once.
Habi spoke French with the writer, Italian with the priests,
Arabic to his countrymen,
and like everyone else, lowly English to us!

The evening, as smooth as the wine we drank, passed without incident.
Leaving, I leaned forward and shook hands across the table
with an Iraqi businessman, a former car salesman.
I tried to straighten, but he held me.
How could I leave without my hand, without my eyes?
This man, twenty-five years my senior,
formed in a culture where age confers rank
and I by comparison a mere child,
a stranger from the enemy camp,
this man, with what passion he improvised,
with what humility he pled:

Tell the American people we are not their enemies.
Tell the American people we love them,
but we must have our lives back!
and let go. And sat down.
But I have yet to straighten,
yet to recover my hand or
my sight.

A Break in the Circuit

Iraq
July, 1999

As though we are guests of this nation,
an arbor of small kindnesses—vine, leaf, and tendril—overspreads us.
Nothing random about it.
I drink more tea in two weeks than in forty years.

We walk through a desert
and wonder each day at the deft hands of custom and history
shaping the vine
and the fragrant and rock-bred bloom of Iraqi hospitality it bears.

In Baghdad, a businessman tells me:
Hospitality is in our bones
and waves his hand,
making little of our amazement.
But how does this explain the shopkeeper,
with no hope of a sale,
setting up a table, chairs, hot tea, and biscuits
while we wait for an art gallery next door to open?

Or a much larger gift
from Iraqi mothers at hospitals
of welcoming us into that most intimate space
where they are saying goodbye to their children?
Even confiding in us: *My first child. She was full of smiles . . .*
He got sick from water in the infant formula. I tried to breast-feed
but there was no milk . . . Sometimes food ran out
and we had to skip a meal . . . Sajar is my seventh child.
His brothers and sisters have all died . . .

Right there at the scene of the crime
with evidence everywhere
and forensic experts on hand offering testimony,
a break in the circuit,
a block in the artery of violence.

Amiriya: Shelter or Tomb? The Missile Came to Say

July, 1999

I

Missile

From death to life they raised it, a thoroughbred from an ancient lineage.
In some Pentagonal crypt, from filigrees and fibers and DNA
of colonial monarchs and murderous barons,
they wove its circuitry, its webbed mind,
fitted its depleted uranium skullcap,
and imprinted there, like first thought or first face at birth,
a blueprint of this shelter.
Go home, they said,
and launched it, a basilisk eye.
For blood, a pirate's reptilian heart.
Once launched, let there be in its veins nothing of warmth or light
but made of hunger, only a cold hunger for this pit.
Let it be a maker of seasons, they said,
and let that season be death.
Let it be a maker of tombs and hecatombs.

II

Shelter

Finnish design. Multi-leveled, honeycombed,
and like a hive, provisioned:
food and water for twenty-one days;
bunks, three-high, for 1400 people.

Secure.
Ten-foot reinforced cement walls, ceilings, and floors.
Five-ton steel doors, self-sealing when attacked;
like Caesar's seal on Christ's cave,
no entrance or egress for a prescribed time.

22

Well, if there must be war,
let life in this bunker be ordinary as possible:
children at play,
mothers, grandparents, suckling infants,
prayer and song, work and rest.
In short, let it be *home*.

III
Annunciation

Onward in darkness, the first missile came,
annunciatory, a herald, trumpeting hell's angel.
Came and found its mark:
a ventilation shaft like fish gill or whale spout.
It dove, drove twisting through bone,
a false prophet preparing the way,
auguring *death*.

IV
Hole

Death entered here.
Not a reaper who on silent feet follows,
gathering our days,
who one day scatters the chaff of our lives
and bears onward to fiery source
a ripe kernel,
a burning ember, spirit and soul, of self.
No. Sudden, incontestable, nuclear death.

A gaping wound eight feet across,
and after nearly nine years, still suppurating, still dripping dust and rock.
From this ceiling, steel rods thrust down and out

in a compound fracture;
mangled fragments of once viable bone,
now twisted, bent, broken.

My eyes were never meant to see this,
to flare like torch, sudden with knowledge,
like windows, to open on this illuminative dawn,
but like tinder in its box (named *American, middle class)*
to remain cold, untouched,
and far from flintstone truth.

No One Wanted This

for the staff at Basra Pediatrics and Maternity Hospital

July, 1999

No one wanted this:
in even one darkness the light radioactive,
eating a body from within.

No one wanted wards full of young children with long, drawn faces,
children of sad mouths and empty eyes, cradled in their mother's arms,
those omnipotent arms withered, reduced to husks.
No one wanted nuclear children,
children of depleted uranium and chemical fires.
No one wanted the lions on Iraq's national escutcheon
        replaced by a hooded rider.

No one wanted this.
Not their parents
who imagined laughter and song and games,
sounds other than silence.
Not their grandparents who imagined that their play and work and learning,
year after year,
like an atmosphere, would enfold them,
memories like bricks building the earthen walls and familiar floor
        of their lives
and day by day a bed to lay down in and die.

Not the invading Gulf War soldiers
who fondly imagined they were riding tractors,
plowing fields, preparing a bountiful harvest,
returning this garden to Eden.

Not the air force gunners straddling their A-10 Warthogs
who sowed depleted uranium rounds and planted
    cancer forever in air and soil.

Not sailors and pilots who bombed chemical munitions factories,
setting Iraq's air aflame for generations,
distance protecting them,
whose generals and admirals forgot to distribute gas masks
to Iraqi people on their streets and in their homes.

Not well-trained American citizens,
like spectators in a Roman coliseum,
who pounded beers in sports bars in Boston and New York,
while watching war on television
and cheering green flashes on its screen
with shouts of "Rock Saddam!"

Even the foxes in their White House and Pentagon,
sauntering in mirrored banquet halls, admiring their tails,
even they did not want this
when decades ago,
in the sterile light of a surgery,
they linked hands
and in one voice said *Yes*
and stood tremulously waiting
to have their hearts removed and placed on ice
and their brains dipped in the blood of ancient Anglo lords and kings.

You Are Immaterial

Najaf, after a US missile strike
July 20, 1999

In the timelessness of war
and the vastness of this landscape,
identity escapes you.
On one side of this lonely road,
a few dusty adobe houses defy the desert;
on another, a mechanic's shop sits,
and behind it and above, a grain silo and mill.
You approach an edge of a shallow missile crater, near dead center of this road,
and turn three hundred sixty degrees, squinting,
trying to locate a recognizable military threat.
A bunker perhaps, but your eyes find nothing.
In every direction, to the limit of sight, a sandy landscape stretches, flat and indifferent.
And in that silo, only mountains of grain
and great, mechanized molars milling it to flour.
You finger fist-sized pockmarks, knee, chest, and eye level,
in one outer wall of an engineer's house on the silo compound,
the right height for shrapnel from cluster bombs.
Shrapnel lies on the ground, inert and lifeless now,
and black plastic casings too.

Fourteen people killed; eighteen hospitalized.
You think: *This is where journalists burn their press cards,*
where an archaic myth of objectivity,
long preserved under glass
but exposed now to light and air,
collapses, a jar of dust in the desert.

This is where the unbearable,
in one of its multitudinous shapes,
stares at you volubly in the form of a seven-year-old boy,
his right arm severed by shrapnel.
Your encounter is wordless.

You have traveled nine thousand miles—
across continents and oceans, over mountain ranges,
through deserts whose roads are pencil lines in rock and sand,
across lunar landscapes that even vultures avoid,
through customs and cultures—
to stand here at this boy's bedside . . .
and you have nothing to say.
Even the dead have voices.
You can think only of your own seven-year-old child.
How would she cope with a sudden loss of her right arm?
What explanation for terror striking out of a blue sky?
Your tongue is in solitary confinement.

A man on the next bed, a mechanic who survived, is not silent.
Two of my co-workers dead,
and I'll never work again, thanks to this,
pointing to his abdomen, clawed and gouged by shrapnel.
Your President is a coward,
fighting a coward's war,
attacking unarmed people.

And next to him, another mechanic,
a young man with shrapnel in his brain,
paralyzed and unable to talk.
His brother speaks for him:
He was going to be married in two weeks.
Now he cannot walk.

Would you marry someone who cannot walk?
They have killed his future.
He might as well be dead.
What is a man without the future?

All around you,
in shoes, under sheets, under ground,
are human beings,
but you are immaterial.
A one-armed, seven-year-old boy looks right through you.
His black-robed mother,
standing behind his bed,
won't even look your way.

Gamble

Najaf, after a US missile strike
July 20, 1999

We should have expected illusion:
a mid-summer sun's sleight of hand in this desert
or our minds out of sync with our bodies
here on the opposite side of the globe
where for us day is night and night, day.
Within moments of our arrival in this remote place,
a crowd gathered, men and boys welling about us,
an oasis of people, as though people had percolated out of the earth.

Missiles, not surprisingly, make for storytellers.
Everyone had a story to tell.
We stitched them together:
Three missiles, the first right on the road.
Children, a taxi with two passengers, mechanics here in a garage,
all in the wrong place.
People rushed out to help, and then two more explosions
nearby, in rapid succession.

We met the taxi driver later in the hospital,
wounds and bandages pocking his torso, head, legs, arms
as though he'd been trampled by a rugby team wearing steel cleats.
The first explosion injured my passengers. I tried to help,
but then another explosion. There was nothing I could do.
He looked at the floor.

Missiles are great collectors' items too,
and compatible with their accustomed hospitality,
our hosts made us gifts of mashed, leaden shrapnel,
black and yellow plastic casings,

30

and large pieces of a missile's mangled gray outer shell,
some of its two-inch identifying numbers still clearly visible.
Or perhaps, after all, they were only returning
what someone had dropped, what legally belonged to our country.
Like pilgrims leaving an offering,
a silent procession of donors filed past,
and a hideous mound of bomb parts grew.

Someone demonstrated (later confirmed by experts)
how shrapnel fits snugly in its black plastic skin
and how that unit, alongside five others,
embeds in its thick yellow plastic placenta:
siblings, identical.
We estimated seventy-two precocious bomblets in each gray womb,
designed to shed their skin and fly
as this missile bore down and gave birth.

We shuddered in the flaming sun.
Men, young and old, offered personal evidence:
rolled up their pants and their sleeves
and lifted their shirts
to reveal cuts and bandages
or pointed to a house where someone was convalescing:
Come with me. I'll show you . . .

Shortly, we were scattered, each in a separate, large scrum:
four unauthorized, unknown Americans on a foreign playing field,
foreign rules and referees,
a hundred aggrieved Iraqi players
and no reason but their decency
why this shouldn't bloody be our last game.
We gambled on it
and won.

Verdict

Najaf, after a US missile strike
July 20, 1999

Eventually, the crowd parted and a spokesperson emerged,
the owner of the auto repair garage, a stocky Shia Muslim
with a bright red head wrap.
He addressed us in Arabic:

We are accustomed to fire from the sky.
Summerlong, the sun hammers this flat, tin tray of land.
We have found ways to work with the sun.
But this (pointing to a pile of bomb parts),
this is something else,
bloody, unprovoked, premeditated . . .
Why? Why is your government attacking unarmed civilians?
Look at us.
We live like rabbits in holes.
We come out, and they shoot at us from behind rocks.
Why?

Our response, partial, pathetic:
Many people in America are against this . . .

And right back at us he came with:

You live in a free country.
It is not enough to talk.
You must act.

The sentence thus spelled out,
he sent us without ceremony, without forgiveness
on our way.

32

Remembering Omran

for Barbara and Simon

July, 2000

The Earth does not accept your death, Omran.
Soil and air, water and rocks are not mute and blind.
They discern between cataclysm and cataclysm,
between our planet's own seismic upheavals
rearranging landscapes, flattening homes and marketplace stalls,
and these extraterrestrial F-16s tearing the blue paper sky above Iraq,
shattering childhood, and scattering, like wheat chaff on wind, everyday
security.

Earth, who gave birth to you and suckled you,
whose face you walked,
upon whose back you raised your sheep
and played soccer,
who cradles you now
and rocks you into eternity,
does not strangle on her own grief
but speaks to us directly,
bidding us *Remember . . . remember*
—and calling out your name.

Toma

Baghdad
July, 1999

The Palestine Hotel, roomy above the Tigris,
is broad-shouldered and stands tall like a five-star general,
though his glory days are long past and lived now only in memory.
In fact, rattle-headed dementia setting in, old circuitry failing,
the elderly man neglects himself,
only half-embarrassed by incontinence, by rotting teeth,
by dirty hair and disheveled clothes,
the once-popular rooms of his mind rutted in the past, peopled with ghosts.

A dozen times in a week we ate there
and saw only eight other paying customers, but had
the best hummus and flatbread, best lentils in the neighborhood.
Possibly the best waiter, too: Toma.
Who said, apologetically, *This restaurant used to be filled every day.*

Returning battered from a hospital or a bomb site,
we dined, early or late, and always Toma greeted us,
his round, Kurdish face a full moon,
as though he lived there and was welcoming us into his home.
Pride of place, to be sure. Stories of Iraq's prosperous past:
Baghdad, the Paris of the Middle East . . . Basra like Venice.
And the north where my family is from,
a land of mountains and rivers and snow.
Someday you must go there.

For ten days, we had him to ourselves.
On the eve of departure, partway through a late-afternoon meal,
he stepped unbeckoned to the side of our table,
black tie, pressed white shirt, white towel ever over his arm,

34

and formally, as though speaking to an assembly, implored us:
When you get home, please tell everyone what you have seen.
It is not for me—I have lived my life.
It is for my children.

And returned to his post.

Such a small thing to ask, I thought, given the life term
    his children labor under.
A few words on behalf of the prisoners, an appeal for mercy.
But no. He had sized us up exactly, asking neither too much nor too little,
and all delusions we harbored of heroism,
every demented notion of conquest and glory
burned like wood chips in the small fire of his words,
expired suddenly like a broken Baghdad electrical current,
leaving us less and more ourselves.

March to War

The September 11 terrorist attack gave rise to the Bush administration's "War on Terror." In the eighteen months between September 11, 2001 and the invasion of Iraq, millions of people worldwide marched in opposition to a United States war in Afghanistan and the threat of war in Iraq. We know now that these efforts failed to stop the invasion of Iraq and the bloodshed it has caused. At the time, however, people across the United States held fiercely to the hope that war could be averted and a nonviolent resolution to the crisis could be found. Six months before the invasion and just after the one-year anniversary of September 11, I returned to Iraq, again with a fact-finding delegation sponsored by Voices in the Wilderness. On this delegation, I had three goals. First, I wanted to interview Iraqis about the threat of war. Surely, I reasoned, it should matter to us what people in Iraq think. Second, I wanted to investigate the likely consequences of a United States military invasion on ordinary Iraqis. Last, there were a few families in Iraq with whom I'd maintained indirect contact, and I wanted to see them and talk with them and their children.

A Small Act

for Annie

September 12, 2001

That day New York's Trade Towers couldn't stop falling—
the TV networks like drunken saviors,
their long-armed cameras bringing those towers repeatedly back to life,
like dead bodies not allowed to be done
but dragged back through fanged doors to death's bramble bed—
that day we lived only in the moment of impact.
Rescue workers, now dead, had not yet arrived,
though by midday we could see them coming,
like ants to the base of a burning tree
and ready to catch those buildings when they collapsed,
glass falling endlessly as though our sky itself had been shattered,
that omnipresent fireball an apocalyptic eye incinerating our past,
daring us to believe in a future.

What our nation's strongmen believed was clear enough—
This was an act of war.
McCain, Feinstein, Rumsfeld, interchangeable:
different names, same mind
set on *retaliation, retribution.*
Likewise, on their White House steps, Pentecostal members of Congress
gave one homily after another, showing bare steel beneath their robes,
promising to brandish it in battle
and ending, Republican and Democrat hand in hand,
with a rendition of *God Bless America,*
invoking a horse of war.

That morning—while I tried vainly
to reach my brother Christopher in Manhattan, my Aunt Mae in Brooklyn,
prayed for my brother Dan, a police officer downtown—
Annie asked me to speak, on her radio show,

37

the words of a peace activist.
I flew my coop into a nearby tree
leaving words like chicken scratch in dust
too soon . . . too risky . . .
Better to find a better speaker . . .
But soon, afraid of heights, I returned
and cock-a-doodle-dooed my way
through an interview, something like this:

We mourn.
This act of violence, like all violence, a horror.
Large-scale? Yes,
and no: like an ant hill beside a mountain
stacked against that pile of rubble we call the "Gulf War."

Further,
(opening that can,
loosing those snakes)
seeds of hatred sown for decades by US policies and actions
in nearly every region of our world
may have found their flowering today.

Our leaders have pledged to kill this vine with defoliant.
A saner response: self-reflection, remorse, formal apologies.
Thus are new methods of farming undertaken,
new crops raised.

Later, at a local blood bank,
Sherrie and I opened our veins,
offered seeds crammed in those pods
to fill bags for shipment to New York.
A small act,
underlining in red,
a larger act of speaking out.

Words of War

September, 2001

From Washington,
out of drooling, cavernous mouths,
words of war pour like bats from a cave,
a black blizzard.
Who can resist them?

Let the gatekeepers of our hearts beware:
rain in mountains, words fall and collect,
filling creeks,
raising rivers,
threatening to burst levees and dams.

And still words pour.
Who can see through them?
A seventh plague, they hatch:
locusts, they devour our sky, quench our sun,
threaten everything our heart's life depends on.

Calling You Home

*For my brother-in-law Donald,
called to active duty in Afghanistan
and later to Fallujah*

*Peace rally, Fort Bragg, California
September 29, 2001*

Peeling tight-fisted, cold-fingered fog from the heart of the land,
our sun laid down its unambiguous, life-giving glory,
a golden oil anointing sand and sea.
Sea and land looked back,
children, used to harsh stricture,
astounded by love.

Taking our sun as model and mentor,
we laid down
like lifeline
or linked hands in a dark passage,
our bodies on the grass outside Town Hall

while singers and poets laid down their words
and drums, their rhythms.

Then altogether,
in song-filled procession through downtown,
laid down our feet, one in front of another,
marking time,
marking pavement visibly, invisibly.

Sum at day's end?
We laid down our hearts
like a body of a song or poem calling you,
like footprints marking the only way safely home.

The Earth Countered

February, 2003

By now we know it began months, even years ago, high above tree line
with a mere tic or twitch
or more likely deep in that mountain's core
a shudder manifesting itself in a falling shelf of ice and snow.
Early on, few people outside Iraq heard or noticed
as snow sped, gathering momentum and mass,
multiplying itself, possessed and possessive, consuming trees and boulders,
growing, growing,
an avalanche of war, a lunatic descending on Iraq,
a nation of twenty-four million people, birthplace of civilization.

Determined to do its worst,
history chose a new breed of reptiles,
Cheney and Rumsfeld and Rove,
crocodiles with keratinous horns, rhinoceroses with
    carnivorous teeth and jaws,
and vomited them onto its calamitous battlefields,
and one more person: Bush,
their blue-eyed Texas lupine,
their fanged smile, poisoned goblet, whining wolf,
an adolescent for an adolescent age.

Earth countered with a million people
and millions more in its streets crying *No!*,
and a mere man, an Austrian alpinist,
a diplomat with a worker's stocky build,
hard-thinking, plain-speaking Hans von Sponeck.

The wolf counseled war to end all threat of war,
promised peace through chaos, freedom through occupation.

41

The crocodiles offered preemption.
Gorgon lunacy propagated, bearing down upon Baghdad.
But itinerant Hans, nobody's fool, played the fool,
trekked our globe and preached a way out.
He cried *dialogue!*   *international weapons inspections!*   *law!*
shaped his lips in a circle and cried *hope,*
spoke, for any who would hear, *sanity.*

The Whole City Sees It

San Francisco rally against the war
January 18, 2003

The people roll toward San Francisco
as raindrops run in mountains,
merging, swelling,
racing for lower land.

Eight busloads from Grass Valley,
twenty from Los Angeles,
thirteen from Sacramento and Davis.
From every city and hamlet, rivulets into creeks into rivers
until a great confluence of waters at Justin Herman Plaza
swells Market Street River to flood stage.

A thunder of waters echoes through urban canyons and gorges,
among high steel and glass cliffs.

Two hundred thousand droplets become one lithe body,
one voice proclaiming, one song announcing
an end to war and talk of war,
a start—can you believe it?—of something new.

Later, weary, we make the long trek homeward.
From the Golden Gate Bridge, like Pharaoh's right hand
or George Bush's,
a round red moon rises above the cracked brow of the horizon.
The whole city sees it.
The whole city watches as,
silent and unapologetic,
it pulls a white silk glove
over its blood-stained palm.

Leaving for Iraq

for ten-year-old Rachael

September 19, 2002

This isn't terror,
that anything-but-blind stampede of fear.

Every child, of course, knows terror,
the cliff edge and free fall beyond,
the unmediated, merciless rocks below.

But this—

Rachael's unstanchable tears;
Rachael clinging to me like a drowning child,
her inconsolable *No!* a last word I hear
walking out our door, a dark send-off.

No, this is not terror.
This is grief.

Terror I would meet in Iraq.

An Eternal Present

Baghdad
September, 2002

We left North America and cruised under clear skies
at thirty-five thousand feet,
eternity everywhere, our small plane at its center.

This is one way to write history.

In this time warp known as Iraq,
we find a different aspect of eternity presiding:
an eternal present,
unbounded, falling away forever in every direction.

What we normally refer to as present
is that thick, elastic membrane between our oceanic past and future,
that shallow, protected lagoon we wade into each morning.

But here in Iraq, that membrane is so thin, so porous,
people routinely travel forth and back,
like shamans, bringing news.
Prophecy abounds.
At a Basra hospital yesterday, Dr. Assad Essa reported matter-of-factly,
Sanctions are a form of occupation.
We live with our hands tied behind our backs . . .
Soon we will trade sanctions for an invasion.
If it is not today, it will be tomorrow.
Our hands will still be tied.

And this afternoon at Baghdad University,
the dean of its law school tore that membrane in two.
We tread deep water.

The US will find a pretext to attack.
It will either be weapons of mass destruction
or support for terrorism.
No proof will be given.
No proof is needed because America operates
by the law of the strongest.

And if the US military stays, we asked?

Then we will move, he said,
kicking the torn membrane under his desk,
from occupation
to occupation.

Classes in Citizenship

Basra
September, 2002

Living in Iraq,
hearing rabid waters,
seeing their foaming jaws, furious teeth,
who can resist trembling?

The blood-blind river of sanctions,
apparently at permanent flood stage,
swollen with lies and deaf to reason,
swallows trees and homes,
drags children under
and scatters their remains on its banks.

Young bones burn white in a desert sun.
All night they glow, luminous as stars or minds.
Day and night, in perfect American Sign Language,
they teach each other to tie their shoes,
to speak English,
to quote the Bible,
to pledge allegiance.

There is so much to learn.

The Beast in Baghdad

Baghdad
September, 2002

We saw the Beast again in Baghdad,
second time in two days.
No, not Saddam Hussein, his presidential smile
only half concealing the armaments behind his eyes,
but a deadlier menace:
depleted uranium, cold and unadorned.
On cots in wards and on chairs in hallways,
children sat, slowly roasting,
leukemia a fire in their bones and blood.

A child has a ninety percent chance
if she gets the correct regimen of medicine,
Dr. Faruq told us. *But at any one time,*
we typically have only three of the five medicines
required to treat leukemia.
This is because of sanctions.
So we mix and match,
administering whatever we have on hand.
It's a losing game.
You see the results here in front of you ... and at the morgue.

We stood next to Zaineb's bed.
A naturally social child greeted us with a toothy smile.
That smile,
her shining hair and polished brown eyes,
the bright orange dress below,
all belied her dark secret.
Every thirteen-year-old should have a secret, right?
Her doctor brings it to light.

This child's cancer was in remission.
Now she has had a relapse.
Once there is a relapse,
chances of recovery drop to five or ten percent.

Later, as we packed ourselves into a taxi outside a hospital main entrance,
ready to sail off,
a woman thrust herself into our car through a passenger side window,
arms, head, torso,
and in her hands, medical reports.
The late-summer heat was no match for her.
For half an hour she remained like this, inescapable,
an anchor binding us purposefully to that spot,
telling the story of her son's illness
and pleading that we do something for him.
In the end, we accepted the papers,
a half promise,
a dishonest *We'll see what we can do,*
and said goodbye,
knowing there was nothing we could do.

Next morning, at breakfast in our hotel's small restaurant,
before food reached us,
before even coffee was poured,
a man approached our table,
an emissary, it turned out,
from the woman who'd held our car at the hospital.
He nodded toward the street.
We followed his gesture with our eyes
to see her standing at curbside in front of a taxi.
We saw her child, limp in her arms.
We heard the Beast roar.
We smelled its foul breath.

49

Kathy Kelly

December, 2002

Multi-colored and refracted,
light from those pilgrim eyes
is a thousand shards of glass,
a rainbow.
Gathered at night at risk,
decanted a hundred times,
stored under pressure,
that light is contraband carried undeclared
through customs
around our globe.

Trace it,
trace it to its source:
in a desert,
in hospitals,
in pediatric wards,
on beds,
burning in ten thousand Iraqi mothers' eyes.

Bert Sacks

Baghdad
September, 2002

Midlife, without fanfare or fuss,
as though it were commonplace,
he traded his engineering career
to become a tree
and, spreading his limbs,
found he could span our globe,
Seattle to Basra.

Citing obscure agricultural ordinances, travel restrictions,
and traditional pest control policies,
federal government officials threatened to cut him down.
They cordoned off a space around him
and gunned their chain saws.
In response, he summoned wisteria and wild roses to climb his trunk,
orchids to hang from his limbs,
endangered species to nest in his branches.

Editors, journalists, and members of Congress
sip coffee in the ample shade of his arbor.
A steady shower of words like infinite leaves falls upon them,
configurations of leaves like runes directing them to Baghdad,
to Basra.

Iraqi children,
healthy or ill,
move in his branches,
climb on vines, clothe themselves in flowers.

On a Day When

Basra
September, 2002

Who needs a map in Basra,
the economy lying uprooted,
the city hoarse and breathless under a banner of malignant air?
Here, every person is a clue
and every encounter is an X marking the landscape
and inviting us to *dig here.*

On a day when the sun got stuck in its rounds
high and hot overhead—

when mercury, from climbing, grew lightheaded and asthmatic,
finally stalling in the stratosphere at 123 degrees Fahrenheit—

when we had already spent three hours in a hospital
visiting children burning with leukemia or typhoid,
their season of heat and humidity never ending—

we waded out of the Basra Sheraton
and into the liquid, noontime air,
walking slowly like cardiac patients through chest deep water
from one end of a pool to another.

Three shoeshine boys who worked the hotel
and slept on its lawn each night
flagged us. We knew them by name: Hassan, Ali, Raed.
Look what we have, they beamed,
their eyes drawing us into an incandescence brighter than sun.
Inside a cardboard box, of all unexpected things, an injured pigeon
captured with a slingshot.

52

The pitiful and terrified creature,
a bloody symbol for Iraq itself, we thought,
lay on its side breathing laboriously,
head twisted and neck bent grotesquely,
struggling in vain to work its wings and right itself.
We'll keep it alive, they told us,
until nightfall.
Then, meat for dinner!

Fresh Air

Baghdad in the thirteenth year of sanctions
October, 2002

In surreal Baghdad,
ash and smoke from the volcanic threat of war
infiltrate the diesel pall smothering the city
and mix with the denser effects of sanctions
already poisoning the air,
coating our lungs,
an acid, metallic taste on our tongue.

Weeks? Months? Who can say when the mountain will blow,
when battering tsunami waves of artillery will land.

Meantime, we walk streets,
ducking into a music store on a main drag.
Not compact disks and cassettes but Middle Eastern instruments.
Danny picks up a flute, conjures
bird song, forests, water over river rocks.

Tamal, store owner and friend, plays for us
one after another: oud, doumbek, flute, tambourine,
a one-string Bedouin violin with an unpronounceable name.
Singing in Arabic, sinuous and sensual,
he draws us delightfully in.

We breathe deeply an hour in a cramped store,
Tamal making love to us,
music cleansing the air,
a series of no-trail, paper-free transactions
no Sanctions Committee can touch.

All in a Good Day's War

Flying from Baghdad to Basra
September, 2002

Nothing could have been easier,
as though they'd chartered a private jet for us
and for a few other local or visiting luminaries.
A private airport, too,
for in all that cavernous, metropolitan port,
ours was the only flight scheduled.
More like a mortuary than a commercial center,
a trade in death, perhaps.
Appropriate, since death is the number one commodity here.

Once airborne,
we succumbed to familiarity and its narcotic magic
and flew comfortably unaware through any threat of war,
forty-five minutes through the "southern no-fly zone,"
from Baghdad to Basra.
We knew only our airline attendant's solicitude,
our pilot's easy, authoritative voice in Arabic and in English,
reminding me of a carriage ride in a park,
and our plane's assertive self-confidence,
spoken in that universal language
of broad shoulders and internal combustion.

But in Iraq, it's what you don't know
will hurt you—E. coli lurking in tap water,
depleted uranium buried in soil,
unexploded ordnance appealing as a songbird or child's toy,
an F-16 at forty thousand feet eyeing your house.

In our case, an early morning missile attack on Basra airport

only hours before we landed,
striking a mobile radar unit.

Offering further evidence of both how small our world is
and how extraterrestrial Iraq has become,
we learned of this attack only that night from friends in Chicago.

They attacked Basra airport, early morning;
just before you flew in!
Already we've received anxious phone calls
from your family and friends here in the States . . .

And attacked again three days later when two United States Congressmen
were there to visit hospitals and sewage treatment plants,
Congressional business clearly secondary to military business,
at least when they are at odds.
Disarming villagers before you raid their village, Leah said,
getting right to the point of military strategy.
Forget that this is a civilian airport
and that radar is necessary to safe commercial air travel.
Forget that Iraq is a sovereign nation
and any legal framework of "no-fly zone" reconnaissance and engagement
is built of papier-mâché.

No doubt that pilot observed his missile strike,
then pulled his reins, and leaning into its neck
and murmuring into its ear, drove his mount home.
Afterward, no doubt, he reported, *Mission accomplished.*
All in a good day's war.

Nowhere for Your Children to Hide

Basra
September 26, 2002

I recall a crisp February afternoon in California, at sunset,
walking into a garden to bed down our asparagus
against white fangs of killing frost.
Overhead, a snapping of wings erupts
as fifty frantic robins move into dense tree cover
accompanied by cackles and murmurs, a sort of air raid siren
as I had come to learn,
and sure enough, moments later, our resident Cooper's hawk,
a blue-gray-backed, long-tailed accipiter,
glides overhead on routine reconnaissance.
No threat. This time.
But the robins, taking no chances,
have already become so many black and orange leaves in the forest.

This image ultimately fails.
Here in Basra,
when air raid sirens raise hackles and heart rates,
no one moves,
no one flees for cover.
There is, quite simply, nowhere to run,
nowhere
for your children
to hide.

Hammer Throw

Basra
September 27, 2002

The sun, that burly Olympian athlete,
pivots in her thrower's circle and spins counterclockwise,
back bent, arms outstretched, shoulder sockets straining
against the centrifugal weight of the ball,
but she never releases the hammer.

What if she let go and the Earth drifted out of orbit,
into cold, into diminishing light?
How long would we last?

How long before our fireplace consumed our minds,
before we worshipped it,
installing it as an altar at the center of our lives,
before new religions arose
and out of the magma of the times, new liturgies formed and hardened,
every ritual designed to enforce the fire?
How long before entire battalions were guarding energy installations and oil
refineries,
before we burned our last chair?

How long would we remain human?
How long before barbed wire bands of fear around our hearts and minds
unmade us
and killing erupted:
a spontaneous battle for our neighborhood's last tree,
for wood in an old barn outside town,
for flammable refuse at our county dump?
How would alliances form,

how would we decide whom to trust,
whom to fear?

I encounter these questions like unexploded ordnance,
while walking in Basra along a sunburst bank of the Shatt al-Arab,
trying to fathom a quickening war.
The river lays itself down as it has always done,
from Turkey to the Persian Gulf.
Forty miles upstream, at Al Qurnah, sheep graze
where Tigris and Euphrates conjoin,
where this river spreads its long legs,
where thousands of years ago it gave birth to human civilization.
Downstream, like a wound, its glistening mouth opens into the Gulf
and not far below that, its cloudy eyes open.
Here, where I now walk, must be this river's breast,
undefended, exposed, its diseased arteries invisible in the turbid flow.

Across the river,
marshes which once supported a way of life unique in this region now
wither.
Drained by Saddam Hussein's government,
a political strategy trumping livelihood and history,
they testify to ancient pathways.
If you rent a boat and float along the far banks, you can see metal gates,
a series of levees which starve these marshes.
You can also see some of their lowland people, "Marsh Arabs,"
who still manage to live off this waterway,
their thatched reed huts, their fishing boats, their barefoot children.
Upstream, center of this river, the rusting carcass of a Cuban cargo ship,
bombed and capsized twelve years ago in the Gulf War,
its freight of food wasted,
floats belly up, a dead and hollow whale.
South of this city, tortured oil fields confess their crimes.
Begging for mercy, they scream at night and give up their treasures.

Overhead, US military jets secure their prison.
In Basra, air raid sirens scream daily, mobile radar units explode,
and only last week, in a residential neighborhood, a missile strike killed
eight people.
No one here can escape the fact of war,
a certainty that their Earth is drifting out of orbit.
You don't need to commission a study,
you don't need a PhD,
you don't need a thermometer to know
the temperature is falling.

Until

Umm Heyder's home, Basra
October, 2002

Like a thousand other buildings in Basra,
this one has a concrete slab for a heart,
a sand and gravel soul.

Several branches of a family tree live here:
five bedrooms for twenty-five people,
more warren or warehouse than home,

until Umm Heyder greets you at the door with *Welcome! Welcome!*
her igneous eyes and starburst smile eclipsing a shattered walk and battered
masonry,
her lowland, riverine voice spilling its banks,
clothing their naked rooms with paintings and tapestries,
their yard with vines, flowers, pomegranates . . .

until her husband, whom you've never met,
offers his hand and humbly *This is your house.*

Umm Heyder, literally Mother of Heyder,
a new name, new identity, honoring her older son,
who was killed when a goddamned JDAM (joint direct attack munition),
in the neutered words of an Air Force spokesperson, *went off course* on
January 25, 1999
and exploded in their neighborhood, leveling homes, killing other children,
and badly injuring Umm Heyder's younger son Mustafa.
The problem, that spokesperson continued in the same sterile tone, *has been*
corrected.

61

Four years later, you see Mustafa, shirtless in late summer heat.
You see his misshapen leg and that space where his fingers once grew
before that missile, in its impenetrable wisdom, pruned them at the knuckle.
You see a jagged six-inch scar on his abdomen
where only hours after the missile had violated him
surgeons penetrated his three-year-old body
to search for shrapnel and remove part of his liver.
What you can't see are twisted fragments of metal
lodged like switchblades in his back and migrating toward his spine.
The doctors couldn't remove them.

If a human body long remembers its wounds—
a weight of rocks on Mustafa's chest and legs and crushing his hand—
perhaps, in remote recesses, memory flickering like marsh light,
it also remembers a pressure on his legs and back
where his mother cradled him
as she ran through streets to a hospital.
Perhaps one day this will save him from despair.

But this is a social visit,
and that story has been told and retold,
and you have agreed to stick to other stories.

More children than you can count,
more names and faces than you can track
dance through the room,
an improvisation.
Directing, arbitrating, comforting,
still tending to her guests,
Umm Heyder sits at its center.

For the first time during this visit to Iraq,
time runs on light rails, smooth, nearly frictionless,

62

and you can almost believe
you really are here for only a social visit,
and the threat of war recedes,

until you remember a wrinkled white envelope
containing two thousand dollars collected in the United States.
You will give it to Umm Heyder as you leave and without a word,
as though it didn't actually contain a measure of that most rare commod-
ity—security.
She will use it for a neighborhood emergency medical fund.

Then Umm Heyder herself, sitting beside you, turns and asks:
What is the mood in the United States? Will they attack?

And that train lurches.
Wheels scream and lose their grip,
throwing the near-perfect spinal cord alignment of cars
sickeningly out of shape,
and the war, the war explodes again in your midst.

Look about.
Its wreckage is all around you.

Anger

Basra
September 27, 2002

Anger we'd encountered before.
In private conversations with doctors,
between lines, and amid understatements,
a deep undertow pulled, a heavy drag of futile days.

Or diffuse at a bomb site,
a poisonous vapor contaminating the air,
burning our eyes and throat.

Or fire as from the mouth of an Iraqi journalist
at the press center in Baghdad yesterday:
Of course people are scared!
This isn't a game.
It's war.

But at schools, hospitality reigned,
and there was nothing in the news this month
or in the diminutive frame of this Iraqi woman
to prepare us for the thick and knotted rope
of her wrath.

The last teacher to stand and speak,
Nadia was still lashing us
as we exited the room.

Visiting Ahmed's Family

Baghdad
September, 2002

In a typical, North American fireworks show,
a rocket will climb the night sky and, with a burst of light, explode.
Concussive sound will follow, noticeably delayed.
Here in Iraq, the opposite occurs:
the sound of war before the actual display.

War is the invisible presence when we gather here with friends.
We hear it howl, but who wants to throw a cloak on that specter and give it
form?
This afternoon, we sit on a bare concrete floor in Ahmed's living room.
We are an odd collection of people,
arranged like furniture along the walls:
Ahmed and his four younger siblings, barefoot and brown skinned;
his shy and quiet mother, unsure what to do with her hands and eyes;
Mohammad, a soldier in the Iran-Iraq war, now working as a taxi driver;
and three Americans, recently arrived in Iraq and soon to depart.

A thirteen-year-old shoeshine boy, Ahmed is the family breadwinner.
A small boy with large responsibilities, he is proud to have us visit.
Such power we have to please.
We give Haider and Jamal, eight-year-old twins, a fistful of Iraqi dinars.
They return with soda sold in old Coca-Cola bottles.
Our throats tingle as cold, dark bubbles burst.
We savor the pleasure.
We savor the moments together,
a brief time out of time.

I step outside with Haider

to kick a deflated soccer ball in the rocky yard.
For half an hour we are two boys with a ball,
defying time, celebrating the present moment.
Beyond us, the Saddam City ghetto breaks like a wound, oozing in every direction.
Somewhere in the Persian Gulf, battleships gather.
I cannot yet see how brightly Haider's future will flash,
but as I put the ball down and prepare to leave,
I can hear its concussive blast.

They Listened

Baghdad
September 25, 2002

The green grass and lush garden—
flowers, figs, date palms, fountains—
were a benediction, a sparkling beverage.
Our born-again eyes,
only hours before interred in a Baghdad pediatric ward,
drank deeply.

Five hundred varieties of dates, our host, Quassim, said,
five hundred different names.
One huge one is called donkey's balls.
He grinned, shaping his upturned right hand as though holding a mango.

The spread of appetizers, shrimp cocktail to dates,
rich in any country, is like a dream or fairy tale here
and with a dark thread running through it:
we heard labored breathing of malnourished children in our ears,
and their eyes pleaded like fingers,
a light touch from behind on our shoulder: *remember me?*

An ancient culture here, Quassim said
from across a four-foot, wrought-iron fire ring.
On three of six iron spikes, he had impaled a whole bottom fish,
each one upright and its mouth to the next one's tail fin,
as though swimming ring-around-the-fire,
but caught in its teeth and slowly roasting.
A style of cooking five thousand years old.
They have the paperwork to prove it.

Light from that fire danced in his eyes.
European wine danced there too.
We didn't ask where he got this wine. We drank it.
You like it here? Why not buy a home in Baghdad.
Prices have never been better!
We didn't ask where he got his good cheer or vigor
in a country forbidden to import necessary raw materials.
We basked in it and in that glowing fire.

No one is having gallery openings any more.
They say it's not worth it, no one comes . . .
Pah! They've given up . . .
Fuck them all, he said, laughing.
I have an opening next week.

We moved to his gallery.
Forty-nine sculptures and paintings for sale,
a range of known and lesser-known Iraqi artists.
They are after Saddam Hussein because he spits in their faces.
He spoke the forbidden name,
spoke it matter-of-factly.
This is nothing new.
Clinton tried to get him, too . . .

But I tell you this, his eyes burning with more than wine,
if war comes,
I will send my family to Jordan,
and I will stay here
in my yard
with my Kalashnikov
and guard my home.

Across that city, across that region,
women stood still, stopped breathing.
Young men and old leaned toward us:
with one body, one mind they heard.
And those children perched on my shoulder breathed deep,
gained weight.
They cocked their tiny ears.
They listened.

Another Day

On the highway to Baghdad
September 22, 2002

Where else but Baghdad can you catch a cab ride
and renew the prescription for your blood pressure pills at the same time,
and both for less than two dollars?

Where else but Iraq do you find incognito engineers and
　　doctors driving taxis,
pilots come permanently to ground in front of hotels and selling cigarettes,
born-again high school math teachers
sitting cross legged in city marketplaces like capitalist gurus,
a prayer shawl in front of them lined with batteries,
plastic flashlights, and kerosene lamps to light the
　　darkness during inevitable brownouts?

A hospital's chief doctor told us:
There are many reasons why we are short staffed.
We need doctors, yes, but if you want to make money in Iraq,
you drive a taxi or sell cigarettes.

In the late 1980s our friend Sattar had a new marriage, a young family,
and coursework in civil engineering promising a good job.
Like laboring through a cut in mountains, steep and narrow,
but soon, surely, soon their future would open onto vistas
where below would lay a wide and sunny valley with fruit trees and gardens,
a river flowing through it feeding melons, vegetables.
In short, prosperity and comfort . . .

Until war and acid-raining sanctions

blocked their pass with boulders and poisoned their water and soil.
The damage was complete. Iraq's derailed economy lay,
shattered and burning, at the bottom of a gorge.
Sattar climbed out and found himself unemployed in a
        nearly jobless landscape
and responsible for extended family, also without income.

By the mid-90s he had two children,
and always now, like snake under rock, a threat of disease lurked
and a lack of money like burnt air choked him.
In the midst of this, a window opened: a job driving wealthy clientele
between Baghdad and neighboring countries, especially Jordan.
The choices one is forced to make:
despite evident dangers—
thieves, kidnappers, crazed drivers, endless hours behind the wheel—
despite time away from precious wife and children,
he accepted, for what is the future but a dark hole, a snake pit,
without some means to move ably through the present?

What Sattar has done for us at Voices in the Wilderness—
rock steady he ran that two-lane gauntlet between Amman and Baghdad,
shepherding small groups of Americans through customs, past its wolves,
our trucks, loaded with sheep, untouched,
and trips to Mosul and Kirkuk, to Najaf and Amara and Basra.

And more: he risked fines and arrest,
time and again breaking a Jordanian law that prohibits foreign drivers,
by coming into Amman, right to our hotel,
to load, in darkness, contraband medicine and supplies.

When once asked,

When you drive us to a hospital,
why do you wait outside?
Why don't you come in?
Sattar responded, eyes averted:
I don't like to see these children, sick and crying,
and no help for them.
I have four children at home.
Who can say whether tomorrow one of them will be sick?
And where will the medicine come from?

A knack for bringing up certain discomfiting historical facts.
Said to me last night in Amman,
For twelve years now, since the Gulf War,
the people of Iraq don't know what will happen the next day.
We do not know what will happen to our children.
Will they get sick? Will there be a bombing?
And now, will there be an invasion?
For us, the war has never ended.

At our hotel this morning, loading trucks, Sattar was all business,
but now, beyond Amman, he strikes another tone
and offers brief, personal stories,
a foretaste, I think, of what lies ahead.

Each year, before school starts, we try to buy clothes for our children.
This year, Marwan, our oldest, says, "I do not need new clothes.
I still have clothes and shoes from last year,
and besides, when the war starts, they will close our schools."
And this is from a ten year old!

Soon, another story about Marwan.
Last week, at home, she asks me:
"Daddy, when you travel,

72

when you go to Amman,
what if something happens here in Baghdad
and war starts?
What will you do to help us?
What will we do?"
And I did not have an answer for her.

And a little later:
I die a death every day not knowing what will happen.
And I did not have an answer for him.

Straight ahead, at an impossible distance,
a round sun steps above the horizon, smiling,
promising the world,
clasping this land in a warm, wide-armed embrace.
If distance were time, we could see forever.
To left and right, a landscape emerges, rocky and inhospitable.
Behind us, long shadows of dawn nip at our heels.
We ride in silence through a blistered land toward Baghdad,
shot like arrows into the sunrise
into another day in the death of a nation.

The Sky Is Falling

Iraq
September, 2002

I

The sky has begun to darken over Baghdad.
You can see it
even through the pall of diesel exhaust crowning its head,
even with your eyes closed.

Soon it will turn yellow, then a yellowish green,
and clouds, slowly at first and without a sound, will begin to rotate,
something clouds should never do,
and just before it falls you will wonder at the massive hulk of the sky
and why you never noticed before how it hangs so ominously overhead.

II

Driving through Fallujah,
Sattar points out construction underway on a roadside,
new homes at this edge of town.
They've stopped working here, he informs us.
No one wants to build a house
just to have it bombed.

What do you make of a country, Barbara offers in disgust,
that shuts down another country's economy?

The wolf, Sattar says, *is big enough to blow down*
even a brick house.

III

The air, saturated with resignation,
coats windshields and the eyeglasses of old people
sitting outside shops smoking in early morning.

74

It bends heads and backs, presses on shoulders.
Life gave up its last surprise long ago.
There is nothing left to do.

IV
Tonight Danny and I swap smiles and stories
with shop owners on Karrada Street in upscale, commercial Baghdad.
Business is poor, they tell us.
People are nervous, waiting for war . . .
They're buying water and kerosene
not watches and jewelry.

On a street corner, an improbable sight.
Alongside their mobile, fast-food cart,
enterprising Iraqi youths have set up a neon McDonald's sign:
unsanctioned falafel sandwiches under the golden arches.

Nearby, in a store, we buy pirated CDs for fifty cents,
supporting our *enemy's* economy,
breaking a US sanctions law
that could shackle us with ten-thousand-dollar fines.

I try to protect my children from all talk of war, the owner says,
but who can do this?
At school, children repeat what they hear at home.
And now my eight-year-old son asks me in the morning,
"Daddy, is today the day we are going to die?"

Cover your heads.
This war has already arrived.

War and Occupation

The US military invasion of Iraq on March 18, 2003 raised more questions than it answered. How would the US military be received in Iraq? Would an occupation ensue or a quick transition to a new Iraqi government? How would the US treat Iraq's cultural and civilian infrastructure? What would it do to protect innocent civilians, especially if fighting moved to urban areas? What kind of resistance would the invading forces encounter? What would emerge in the political aftermath if the US toppled Saddam Hussein's regime? Was civil war really a possibility? Was democracy? Would Iraq fracture along religious lines? And though some of these questions have been answered, the long-term consequences of the invasion and occupation are only beginning to be glimpsed.

The invasion also raised questions for the millions of people who had publicly protested the build-up to war. "What do I do now? How do I remain involved? And what good will it do?" Taking a public stance against war by marching and protesting prior to the invasion, people had become personally involved. This looming threat of war, though so distant, had become personal to people. Marching alongside others, we had also joined a community. Personal commitment was strengthened and supported by community involvement. Somehow, in the aftermath of the invasion, this sense of personal involvement and the urgency it engendered were lost.

Where there was clarity of purpose before the invasion, for many Americans who opposed the war there was now chaos and uncertainty. At times of moral and political crisis, many people turn to art to help make sense of the world, both to give expression to the chaos people experience and to point a way out of it. I turned to poetry. After the invasion, I continued to work with Voices in the Wilderness and to write poetry about events related to the war in Iraq. Because a poem is conceived and born from deep within, writing kept me personally engaged, personally involved. Through writing, events ten thousand miles away remained personal and relevant and thus urgent.

I Wish—Letter to Sattar

March 18, 2003

Sattar, I wish I could say that those North Americans and Europeans
who came like refugees to your country,
empty handed, illiterate, stupefied by travel,
whom you ferried safely forth and back
across the jagged ocean of rock and sand between Jordan and Iraq,
even as winds increased and stone fists rose,
even as that lunatic storm, raving and possessed
and implacable as a fire, approached,
all the while your precious children directly in its path . . .

In Iraq, we landed panting like migratory birds blown off course,
nearly imperceptible dots on a swirling, urban landscape,
driven from our homes by a bubbling cauldron of war
about to boil over.

O! didn't your country clothe and feed us with its passion for justice,
its intelligence, its terror, its outrage—
didn't it befriend us?
Didn't a strong wind carry us home?

I wish I could say that wave upon wave
we landed in North America and Europe
crashing their shores,
and joining others arm in arm
like a tsunami we rose and spread the Earth
taking with us everything—
ears, fences, newspapers, media outlets, microphones,
     government buildings—
and drowning every corridor of power,
we swamped those flames.

O, I can call you *comrade* and *brother*,
and we did rise in numbers,
and, yes, *we will continue this struggle*,
but I wish I could declare with Marxian confidence, like Neruda,
that grain will grow in your country,
that electricity like blood will flow uninterrupted,
rich arteries of power and light pulsing,
that nothing will fall from your sky except sunshine and water,
and rivers run clean to your faucets,
that your children will grow like stalks
in a vast, sun-drenched field of wheat,
their minds like small stars gathering to themselves
planets, moons, atmospheres
their heads crowned with swollen kernels of light.

But no. War, that great gray glacier,
marches from the north,
carrying lightning and thunder, generating its own weather,
grinding and scraping, freezing your economy, crushing everything in its
path.
Who can say, besides destruction and death,
what will follow
and whether I'll ever see you again?

Seeing Sattar Again

May, 2005

Sattar, after two-and-a-half years,
static electric uncertainty mounting month after month in my body,
not knowing whether war had eaten your heart or your mind
or one of your beautiful young children,
seeing you still alive here and now in Berkeley,
and intact,
lightning should have flashed when we embraced,
and laughter like thunder cracked
when we spoke.

Though a world apart
and born to different mothers
and a different mother tongue,
surely we are brothers,
your black hair and bronze skin
a perfect complement
to my northern inheritance,
yang to my yin,
fire to my water,
day to my night.

How else explain this tear in my heart,
this sickening internal bleeding,
after talking with you here on American soil?
The rivers of northern California lash their tails,
our robust mountains burst,
boasting oaks, firs, redwoods
and north and east of San Francisco, they are newly crowned with ice and
snow.
Our Bay Area bridges, never bombed,

79

but hammered by goddesses and gods,
they bind this land and bless its inhabitants,
while Baghdad,
like a car abandoned on the side of a road,
is picked apart.
The first bold strike removes its tires,
and the game is on: hood, fenders, windows . . .
everything of value exposed, looted.
Your city, your country set on blocks
and a sign in English declaring, *all takers welcome*.

Dancing on Iraqi Graves, an Election Night Report

November 3, 2004

There was plenty to celebrate.
As Ohio tipped, bottoms up,
mooning the rest of our nation,
tipping election scales in favor of George Bush,
corks flew and wine bottles also tipped:
pure California sunshine sparkling in glasses,
bubbling in Republican brains.

The walls and ceiling had eyes:
in every corner a surveillance camera peered.
Scattered among those revelers
Secret Service agents secured that ballroom.

All night they danced,
celebrating this war president's re-election.
Meanwhile, below ground, in graves beneath that dance floor,
Iraqis, buried alive and struggling to breathe,
clawed earth and rock like gophers,
seeking a root of their interment.

But not one claw splintered that dance floor
to trip not one righteous dancer.
Eye witness statements support this,
as does incontrovertible evidence
burned on film.

Shock and Awe

January 1, 2003

Today is a good day to remember bombs,
timed to convene mid-March in Iraq:

conventions of bombs
to replace academic conventions
and business conventions
and music festivals
and pilgrimages.

Good to remember that day you first heard bombs whirring overhead
migrating determinedly above your neighborhood, above your home
heading to Baghdad and Basra and Mosul:

flocks of bombs to replace flocks of sheep,
flocks of birds,
children flocking to and from school.

Or perhaps you've heard nothing
only felt pain in your ears at a sudden loss in air pressure,
a drop in temperature,
a cold hand around your heart.

A good day to imagine bombs arriving in Iraq,
crowds cheering,
smiling faces on streets and in windows,
outspread arms, a shower of flowers,
brown fingers shaping V signs:

a parade of bombs
to replace parades of people to marketplaces,

parades of tourists and pilgrims,
the parade of prosperous days and seasons long past.

A good day too to wake from dreams of parades
to a nightmare of roofs caving in,
showers of glass,
living flesh searing, bones splintering,
families shouldering their blankets and baskets
and heading for caves in mountains, seeking refuge,
children shivering in frozen air.

A good day even to remember that it is your flesh,
your bone,
your shoulders,
your hungry children.

New Strategy in This War without Borders

November, 2004

In the Iraqi theater of the absurd,
this war without borders goes nuclear.
Fallujah is made uninhabitable,
transmogrified into Hiroshima minus the mushroom clouds,
a whole city hung from a tree.

While people worldwide take notes, slowly learning
that though you can bomb an insurgency into existence
you cannot bomb one out of existence;

while people everywhere stand slack jawed in horror;

while the Iraqi resistance dons sheepskins
and sneaks out a cave entrance,
heading for hideouts in Ramadi and Mosul,

the United States military Cyclops,
applying its singularly bloodshot logic,
rampages across western Iraq,
trampling people, homes, and hospitals
and shepherding the very terror it aims to devour.

Experiments in Freedom

January, 2005

The results are in.
That same day in mid-January when ornamental almonds blossomed,
drawing bees on the west side of town into dizzying and deeper rings of
ecstatic delight
and bearing witness in northern California to a forward rolling wheel of
Time,
a world away in Iraq, five Kurdish children and three American soldiers
were drawn into another sort of stasis,
fused by a searing experience and tied to it inextricably,
effectively frozen together in time.

A Pentagon spokesperson scoffed at critics
who condemned a practice of using subjects without consent.
Whenever we raise the level of Knowledge,
personal freedom follows naturally.
There's a spillover effect, a symbiosis.

Privately, sources say,
there were "high fives in hallways,"
with one jubilant physicist overheard proclaiming,
We did it! We stopped Time!
But publicly, lead scientists at the Pentagon and White House
greeted test results with cautious optimism,
pointing to our President's inaugural address
as an indication that further research on this matter is planned.

Lines Written in Footprints on Piazza Stones

The mourners speak after the killing of Nicola Calipari
March 4, 2005

How we longed to celebrate,
to be launched into a blue pool of sky,
and like goddesses or gods to bathe in that light.
Every cell in our bodies had hungered for Giuliana's release,
for her to surface,
and every day that she lay captive,
as at the bottom of an ocean,
stretched this taut and frayed bowstring of our longing.

A little light, we said to each other. *A little joy.*
In this smothering darkness of war, a chance to breathe again.

Then Nicola found the spot and dove—our hearts raced!
Like a skull around a brain, a rib cage around lungs,
he wrapped her.
Like a sperm whale carrying its precious oil,
their car swam for the surface,
through darkness toward lights of Baghdad Airport.
Up finally from unknown depths,
safe now, safe.

And in our own minds
we too felt the pressure of all those fathoms fall away.
We saw layers of liquid darkness thinning,
turquoise light diffuse above us.
And when US sharpshooters fired their weapons,
eclipsing our sun,
drowning us again in darkness,
it was our temple their bullet shattered,
our blood that spattered Giuliana's camera.

This Much We Know

Lawton, Oklahoma
November 8, 2004

An anadromous spirit brought us here,
against a current to be sure,
up shallow, far-flung streams—

Rudy from Detroit, Farrah from Philadelphia, Bert from Seattle,
Steve leaping waterfalls and boulders on both sides of our continent,
Jerry only just percolating up out of a hole in the
        federal penitentiary system,
his gold-flecked eyes and broad smile
somehow brighter for those seven months underground.

Something, formed in us at birth,
compelled us homeward.

Home? Who knows a way there?

But a clue lies buried here in Oklahoma's desert,
a point of light winking in a dark prison at Fort Sill.
We squint, trying to hold that image close,
but with little success: they deny our access to the prisoner.
Despite collar, vestments, and Bible, they turn even Reverend Phil away.
So we relax, let our eyes wander darkness,
and other points appear;
across time and space, other stars—
        Franz Jagerstatter, Ben Salmon, Ardeth Platte . . .
a constellation, a signpost pointing:

                    this way and no other.

Letter To Camilo Mejia

Farrah and Bert, knocking on soldiers' doors in Lawton, Oklahoma
November 9, 2004

Camilo,
in the armored, seven-headed logic
of military justice,
you are pathological,
infectious,
a foreign cell in our national bloodstream,
a virulent disease to be isolated, surrounded, smothered.

We seek no chink in that armor.

Rather,
like scientists gone underground
and gathered in makeshift laboratories,
we seek a pure strain of that virus
and every opportunity to spread it,
hoping, in time,
to help infect the entire body.

The Other Side

Lawton, Oklahoma
November 9, 2004

Eight-foot nutcracker soldiers—
ninety-nine by Rudy's count—
greet us without fanfare, without breaking rank,
mutely, with painted smiles,
their cardinal red pants and royal blue coats
hardly the colors of urban guerilla warfare practiced currently in Iraq.

Other lands, other people, Kathy says, *have dreams too.*
To symbolize this, we shed our skin and insinuate ourselves in those orderly
rows,
indecorous decorations on this great lawn,
each of us holding a three-foot, color photo of a living Iraqi child:
Lawton's Boulevard of Lights alight now
with Rania's, Hassan's, Omar's, Heba's
with Imad's and Duha's and Mahmoud's eyes.

We think of children alive in Iraq today, and our hearts stop:
children born in a battlefield without borders,
children of rubble, born in a time when time no longer matters,
a monstrous present gorging itself on their future.
Their future is a windblown pile of bones in sand,
a dull gray distant sky indistinguishable
from that dull gray sea of violence surrounding them,
no ninety-degree angle where water and sky meet, no horizon beckoning.
It is a weary future, no longer able to hold itself up properly like a wall
for a child's eyes to climb, wondering hopefully
what the view, what the other side
might hold.

Here, Rania and her friends are like children from a parallel universe crazily

89

off course

and thrown through a temporary doorway into our world.

Standing here in unaccustomed safety in Lawton, Oklahoma,

they are bewildered by their surroundings—

undamaged buildings, massive single-family homes,

clean water gushing from fountains.

Bewildered, too, by an indecipherable absence of violence,

and most of all by an uninterrupted ticking of time,

a view, from where they now stand, of a future crammed with possibility,

crammed with promise.

This future is a windswept celestial scroll

or a forest, its brown arms and green fingers holding ten thousand birds

and who can say which song or which color will flare next

or whose name distant stars will write

clearly for one moment on our night sky?

A Global Heart

April, 2006

If court were a curtained room, a secret and honeycombed chamber,
we might hear Saddam Hussein scream as the official torturers broke his body.

If justice were a tooth, if we-the-people were a dog pack,
he might disappear, dismembered,
a chorus of wolfish howls celebrating the kill.

We know we want more than this.
But where to start?

I recall meeting with Tariq Aziz, Iraqi Deputy Prime Minister,
in September before the invasion. A time when an anxious sky held its breath,
when sentinel date palms stood watching, when all of Baghdad waited.

A time, too, when Westerners were suspect,
when our eyes could have been hired to locate the sites of government buildings
and to deposit that data into the empty minds of laser-guided missiles.
We traveled to the meeting blindfolded in a car with blackened windows.

As I see it now, backward in time through the dust and haze of war,
a thin veneer coated that city, a mask of normalcy,
but beneath it, ears pricked, eyes gaped in horror, and minds ran on a single,
     terrible track
as an immense wrecking ball of war swung outward on its taut cable,
the terrible arc of its ascent audible and visible above.

We accepted Aziz's invitation because custom required it,
and because it bore, in a small way, on crucial questions.
Why hadn't Iraq been invited into the Security Council for dialogue and
negotiation?
What could our governments agree on?

The conversation tread on clear common ground: our desire to
        end sanctions, avert war.
Aziz, suspecting the United States of
        conspiring to *manipulate weapons inspections,*
outlined a plan *to assemble an international team of*
        scientists to monitor the inspectors.
Barbara summed the meeting afterward: *He must be*
        blind, talking about scientists.
They're going to flatten this place. And sure enough,
in the first days of the invasion, bombed government buildings burned.

Now, Saddam Hussein stands in court,
the ex-king of a hundred palaces,
the fox who never slept in the same den two consecutive nights.
Now that he is reduced to a mere man clinging to a deadly fantasy,
now that he stands in a bright pool of public scrutiny,
we see more clearly than ever our own government reflected in that pool
and drowning in similar messianic delusions,
addicted to the same violent methods, blood blind,
willing to sacrifice without end other people's daughters and
        sons, fathers and mothers.

We long to see the fantasy laid bare, stripped to its lethal, radioactive core
        and contained,
a circular fence erected around it, signs declaring *Danger!* and seven guards
        posted at its gate.
In our yearning, we join ourselves to people in Iraq, to people everywhere,
a global heart longing to see State greed and arrogance revealed for
        what they are:
a poisonous and bloody sword, polluting the Earth, killing our loved ones.
This is our common ground.
Let's build here.

Some Questions about Torture

September, 2005

When a tortured person dies, does violence die with him?
Does it coat the ceiling and walls of that chamber where he was tortured?
Does it pour like a snake from holes in its floor,
nest, like a spider, in cracks and corners?

And terror and pain?
Are they concentrated in ashes or released into air
when his body is cremated?
Do we encounter them with every breath;
do they lodge like asbestos in our lungs?

Do they move through soil where a tortured woman is buried?
Leaching out of her body, are they absorbed underground
into animal bones and tree branches, petrifying them?
Sifting down with rainwater,
through porous earth,
through unimagined spaces below ground,
do they enter an aquifer?
Do we draw them to the surface when we drill wells?
Do we wash our clothes with them?
Are they in this glass of water I hand to my daughter,
this water which sunlight illumines,
this water which carries life also carrying death?
Are they in our bodies?
Absorbed into our bones and our brains,
are they, even now, petrifying them?

In These Offices

for Penny and Jim

outside the office of Nancy Pelosi, United States House
    of Representatives minority leader
September 26, 2005

Blood runs here in these offices.

Beneath hair spray and cologne, beneath every perfumed word,
beneath hot oil and ink of copier machines and laser printers, you can smell
it.
Beneath spicy air freshener, a sharp odor stings our nostrils
and pricks our brain's primal neural receptors.

Beneath every frozen and crusty layer of rationalization, a warm lake of
blood pools.

Behind marble and maplewood walls stretch thin red lines
where fingers, old and young, have traced them,
where hands, trying to hold on, have failed,
where bodies have fallen and, like wine bottles overturned,
have emptied themselves.

It is spilled blood of migrant farm workers and their families,
of castaway, drug-addicted prisoners,
of invisible people in East LA, Appalachia, San Francisco's Tenderloin,
of our hospitals and schools and playgrounds,
shunted and siphoned,
drawn for massive transfusions into military business
into war and occupation and naked military aid.

It is blood of Palestinian and Iraqi children,
their future slaughtered and, like a fattened sow, upended,
hung from a wire, and drained.

It is our Earth's blood.
It is the blood of our planet's newborn future.

In these offices,
under rugs and floorboards, the red liquid pools and flows:
a bloody aquifer that Congress taps,
scarlet groundwater breaking out from hillsides in springs
and feeding weapons manufacturers and oil companies.

This, too, is a war zone.

Comes a Cleansing War

January, 2005

From an administration that banned body bags,
forbidding soldiers to die in combat;

from a president who fails to attend funerals,
nearly three thousand at last count,
three thousand rocket-propelled deaths,
three thousand flag-draped coffins pocketed
in hard ground,
the earth zippered above them,
out of sight, out of existence;

from whirling depths of dementia
where Iraqi civilians are not only unharmed by this war, but liberated,
ecstatics soaring like pelicans, plowing the sea like dolphins
cut free from a net;

from makers of embedded media,
from purveyors of depleted uranium and cluster bombs,
    comes a cleansing war.
United States' weaponry, PhD in hand, disinfects Iraq,
eliminates tyrannical diseases in its soil,
plants *justice* like a grape vine
and *freedom* a trellis it can grow on.
The President makes a *plea for patience*
as young roots spread their fingers below ground,
taking a firm grip on that land,
and a new shoot, feeling fire in its mind and hunger in its soul,
climbs, according to its nature, skyward,
lifting in triumph its arms to our sun.

Anywhere USA

for Shelby West

May, 2006

A local resident, an American soldier,
died in Iraq yesterday
    and now
no one speaks against the war.

An eleven-year-old girl is fatherless
    but she cannot lay her grief at the culprit's feet.
Her grief is a dead child strapped to her back.

She knows the creature who killed her father.
Every night it steps out of darkness
into the daylight of her dreams,
    but she cannot curse its name,
she cannot exorcise it.

Her anger has no object,
    no pointed purpose.
Her rage is a sword locked in its sheath.
The sharpest phrases die in her, unexpressed.

Adults speak dully of honor and service and heroism.
Meanwhile, the impeccable, honorable war,
    like a mafia don,
snaps its cufflinks,
narrows its eyes,
and, flanked by body guards,
rides our streets in a limousine,
unseen behind dark and bulletproof glass.

A Letter from Your Mother

September, 2005

Jason. Every day I say your name.
Every day my voice sounds in the space your absence creates,
inviting you home,
and my mind, like a jazz soloist, improvises on the theme of your life,
every memory a riff.

I start with your death
and work backward through its dominant chords,
a blues scale of rage and fear,
trying to reconcile the dissonant notes that sounded
during those final days and months.

The cancer that ate your young body was itself a foreign army.
Will we ever know what poison, what chemical or radioactive exposure,
launched that invasion?
The doctors can tell me only that *something happened* in Iraq.
The military will tell me nothing.

Oh, Jason, I want you back.
There are so many memories.
Before you died, even when you were in Iraq,
my memories played *andante*,
whole and half notes in simple four-four time,
and I could handle the tempo, the sharps and flats.

Now, amid such a frenzy of sixteenth and thirty-second notes,
my breath fails, my fingers seize on the horn keys,
and I'm afraid I'll drown.

I want you back, Jason.

Burning Books

May, 2006

Under every rock in a forest, a world without end:
seeds, insects, crustaceans,
spores, roots, gems, minerals,
down, down, down forever
to the fiery center of our earth.
Let your fingers plunge, let your mind wander that terrain
and you are a child again, the first scientist,
an explorer, a mapmaker.

But in human cemeteries, under every marble rock,
something else: a story.
Under Master Sgt. Robert West's tombstone, an interrupted story,
beginning, middle, abrupt end.
Above it, a grieving wife and an eleven-year-old child stand,
never again to hold that book in their arms,
to read its pages, to dwell securely between those durable covers.

Last week, an American soldier in Iraq wrote from Camp Ramadi:
We learn quickly how fragile we are.
Some of us thought we were made of iron
and war would make us stronger,
but we are paper,
paper arms, paper legs,
and Ramadi is on fire.

We honor the beginning and middle.
It's the end we mourn.
And I'll say it, conscious of the line I cross,
it's the end I condemn,
not only the roadside bomb that killed Robert,

but the whole affair, a waste.
A waste of mothers, fathers, children,
of hands and feet, arms and legs,
a waste of minds.
Everywhere among us, broken bodies walk, broken minds stalk,
and below ground, like manuscripts thrown in a fire,
unfinished stories turn to dust and ash.

Cindy Sheehan

July, 2006

Look at me, George.
I'm the oncology lab report,
the malignant truth metastasizing
every time an American soldier is injured or killed.
I'm in your lymph nodes, your bone marrow, your lungs.

Look at me, George.
I'm the murky swamp you paddled into four years ago.
I'm the eight-inch gash in your canoe,
the crocodile stepping off the bank, sliding into water,
disappearing beneath the surface.

Look at me, George.
I'm the Joshua tree, gnarled and spiked,
waving you into the Promised Land.
I'm the bristlecone pine two miles above sea level,
thriving on adversity: you can't outlast me.
I'm the river you can't dam,
the flood you can't check,
the voice with ten thousand faces.

I'm the indelible blood on your hands, George.
Take your gloves off, and look at me.

I'm the pursuer, and you're the prey.

Iraqi Women Are Disappearing

June, 2006

War, like a greenhouse gas,
raises temperatures in the Middle East,
spawning monstrous storms,
causing massive dislocations,
and pushing species to the cliff-edge of extinction.

Women are always threatened during periods of war,
but now, as war changes the climate in Iraq,
women are endangered.

As the secular law's permafrost melts,
a bog of religious fundamentalism spreads across the country.
Women are stoned for wearing makeup,
murdered for teaching at a university,
forced to stay indoors unless accompanied by a man
and hidden behind scarves.

Texas oilmen and western neocons square their shoulders,
stay the course,
and Iraqi women, once the most secure in the region,
disappear—

under knives,
under ground,
behind burqas.

Meanwhile

June, 2006

In comatose Baghdad, where months ago
reconstructive surgeons disconnected the life support,
astonishing evidence of consciousness is
    visible in the "fortified Green Zone."
US doctors, failing to resuscitate their patient,
have embarked on a radical therapy: a brain transplant.
Day and night on the west bank of the Tigris,
thirty-five hundred foreign workers build a colossal US embassy,
complete with more than six hundred dwellings,
a recreation center, a school,
and, for people accustomed to a lavish lifestyle, an American Club.
Immodest as a miracle, imported floodlights illuminate the surgery.
A mechanized army of cranes and pulleys performs the operation,
connecting the complex organ to its blood supply.

Meanwhile, on the opposite bank,
Iraqis live on scraps.
Like rats, they eat and sleep
amid the looted rubble of former government buildings,
refugees in their own country
and witnesses to the gangrenous violence spreading throughout the city.

But even if the rest of Baghdad rots,
the new brain will think and breathe and give commands.
Fifteen-foot-thick security walls surround it like a skull.
New sewage and water treatment facilities, like kidneys, purify its blood,
and its own dedicated source of electricity,
humming a John Philip Sousa march,
massages its neural fibers.

Where Silence Can Have Its Say

for Adrienne Rich

October, 2005

There is no need for words.
There is a bottomless need for words.

No need for a pack of canine words
to drag that flaming body in pieces into our yards,
a stench of molten flesh into our kitchens,
its pyroclastic screams into our bedrooms.
No need for someone to tell us what to feel,
as though our human bodies had forgotten how to register horror,
as though the seismograph stylus had to be operated manually
and from a remote location.

A bottomless need for words:
words like tools clearing underbrush,
uncovering a footprint of culture, of gender, of race and nationality.
Words like hands tunneling into earth,
fingers scratching at soil and rocks seeking hidden roots of hatred,
roots of violence,
roots of privilege,
and yes, somewhere, of nonviolent life,
unearthing histories, personal and communal.

But first, a space.
A space where multiple waves of feelings
can vibrate through us,
a massive initial shock and its inevitable aftershocks.
A space where silence can have its say.

The Iraq War Described to a Child

July, 2006

I
A tornado.
From a window in your home,
you watch it step out of the sky,
as if it were the sky itself,
and touch down
and make its drunken and deafening way into your neighborhood.
It swallows a school, your friend's house, a hospital.
Wind from its whirring blades
lifts the roof above your head and carries it away.

II
Lightning,
striking fire in woods.
At the base of your family tree, grass ignites
and hot orange tongues lick its trunk, climbing toward its canopy.
You hear your cousin scream
as leaves on one side of the tree catch fire.
A flaming branch cracks and falls.

III
A volcano.
Out of its fiery belly,
it spews dead bodies high into air,
mothers and fathers, children and babies.
Bodies pile on top of each other.
You can still see the top of the pile of American soldiers,
even as it approaches three thousand feet above sea level,
but in Iraq, the pile has entered the stratosphere.
No one has measured it,
and no one knows how high it will climb.

Last Word

*with Rachael at the national cemetery in South San Francisco
December, 1998*

This child, at six, is all blossom.
Every cell in her body
is instructing, constructing hope, harvest.

From a hilltop neither Calvary nor Zion,
she surveys this national cemetery.

Her private present, bottomless and unbounded,
confronts the past and future of our species,
like an early spring tasting winter at its heels,
observing autumn on its horizon.

Awestruck, she says: *Gravestones . . . everywhere.*
Look . . . thousands!
Indeed. Row after obedient row, acre upon acre;
the blank, unblinking eyes of the dead;
or teeth perhaps
(human fodder slowly digesting below),
straight as figures in a Pentagon budget,

their sum total monotonous as a metronome
last word   last word   last word

of war.

Dr. Assad Essa with Voices in the Wilderness delegates Leah Wells, left, and Barbara Lubin outside the Ibn Ghazwan Hospital in Basra, Iraq, in September 2002
—photo by David Smith-Ferri

Notes

"The Same Four Words," page 1

Witnesses to the slaying of 24 Iraqi civilians by US Marines in the western town of Haditha say the Americans shot men, women and children at close range in retaliation for the death of a Marine lance corporal in a roadside bombing. Aws Fahmi, a Haditha resident who said he watched and listened from his home as Marines went from house to house killing members of three families, recalled hearing his neighbor across the street, Younis Salim Khafif, plead in English for his life and the lives of his family members. "I heard Younis speaking to the Americans, saying: 'I am a friend. I am good,'" Fahmi said. "But they killed him, and his wife and daughters." The girls killed inside Khafif's house were ages 14, 10, 5, 3 and 1, according to death certificates.
                                                            —*Washington Post*, May 27, 2006

United States Marines could face the death penalty . . . [for] the killing of more than twenty Iraqi civilians in the town of Haditha. The Marines involved have since been rotated back to their home base of Camp Pendleton, near San Diego, California.
                                                            —*The Independent*, May 28, 2006

"Every Iraqi Knows," page 3

Abeer means "fragrance of flowers." She was fifteen years old. The soldiers noticed her at a checkpoint. They stalked her after one or more of them expressed his intention to rape her. On March 12, 2006, after playing cards while slugging whiskey mixed with a high-energy drink and practicing their golf swings, they changed into black civvies and burst into Abeer's home in Mahmoudiya, a town fifty miles south of Baghdad. They killed her mother Fikhriya, father Qassim, and five-year-old sister Hadeel with bullets to the forehead and "took turns" raping Abeer. Finally, they murdered her, drenched the bodies with kerosene, and lit them on fire to destroy the evidence. Then the GIs grilled chicken wings. These details are from a sworn statement by Spc. James P. Barker, one of the accused.
—Robin Morgan, "Rape, Murder, and the American GI," August 17, 2006

"Standing There," page 5

On Wednesday, the US military tracked al-Zarqawi to a house northwest of Baghdad and blew it up with two five-hundred-pound bombs . . . weapons so powerful they tore a huge crater in the date palm forest where the house was nestled . . . The airstrike killed two other men, two women, and a girl between the ages of five and seven who were in the house, but only al-Zarqawi and his spiritual adviser have been positively identified.

—Associated Press, June 10, 2006

"Battlefield without Borders," page 7

A suicide bomber attacked a hospital south of Baghdad on Thursday, killing thirty-four people . . . Hasna Aboud's son, who was due to get married next week, was killed. "My twenty-two year old son was killed while trying to bring me some medicine," she said. "I lost my only son."

—Reuters, November 24, 2005

A suicide bomber detonated his car in a crowd of Shiite mourners north of Baghdad on Saturday, killing at least thirty-six people and raising the death toll in two days of attacks against Shiites to more than 120.

—AP, November 19, 2005

"What I found [in Baghdad] was a virtual ghost town, where residents are afraid to leave their homes after dark and heavily armed militias roam the streets."

—Kurdish journalist Ayub Nuri, April 26, 2006

"A Break in the Circuit," page 20

The number one killer of children in Iraq is diarrhea brought on by water-borne bacteria.

—UNICEF, 1998

Access to potable water in Iraq is 50% of what it was prior to economic sanctions.

—World Food Program, 1998

"Amiriya: Shelter or Tomb? The Missile Came to Say," page 22

In July 1999, I visited the Amiriya bomb shelter in Baghdad. Eight and a half years earlier, on February 13, 1991, two very smart bombs struck the shelter and incinerated more than four hundred people, mostly women, children, and the elderly. The first missile, laser guided, found the shelter's Achilles heel: a ventilation shaft. The concussion created by this missile caused the five-ton steel doors to lock automatically, a feature intended to protect the people inside; but in this case it proved deadly. A second missile, entering through the hole created by the first, exploded inside, raising temperatures within the shelter to over two thousand degrees. In Baghdad, bombing raids were typically run at night under cover of darkness, and people would leave the shelter in the morning to return home. Given the extensive reconnaissance that United States warplanes carried out over the city, there can be no doubt the United States military knew from the movement of people in and out of the shelter each day that it was being used to house people not armaments.

"Remembering Omran," p. 33

Suddenly out of a clear blue sky, the forgotten war being waged by the United States and Britain over Iraq visited its lethal routine on the shepherds and farmers of Toq al-Ghazalat about 10:30 a.m. on May 17. Omran Harbi Jawair, 13, was squatting on his haunches at the time, watching the family sheep as they nosed the hard, flat ground in search of grass. He wore a white robe but was bareheaded in spite of an unforgiving sun. Omran, who liked to kick a soccer ball around this dusty village, had just finished fifth grade at the little school a fifteen-minute walk from his mud-brick home. A shepherd boy's summer vacation lay ahead. That is when the missile landed . . . crashing down in an open field two hundred yards from the dozen houses of Toq al-Ghazalat. A deafening explosion cracked the silent land. Shrapnel flew in every direction. Four shepherds were wounded. And Omran lay dead in the dirt, most of his head torn off, the white of his robe stained red.

—*The Washington Post*, June 16, 2000

In the summer of 2000, members of Voices in the Wilderness visited Omran's family at their home outside Najaf. Later that summer, graphic artists at the Middle East Children's Alliance purchased and decorated an old school bus and collaborating with Voices in the Wilderness, launched the "Remembering Omran Bus Tour." The bus, a sixty-foot traveling billboard, crisscrossed North America, traveling eleven thousand miles that first year, bringing speakers who had recently been to Iraq to share their knowledge and experience. The following autumn, after September 11, the bus was redecorated and renamed "Wheels of Justice." Bringing information about conditions in Palestine and Iraq and opposing war and occupation in these countries, it continues to travel across the continent.

"Words of War," page 39

We are coming after you, and let God have mercy on you, because we won't.
—Arizona Senator John McCain, September 12, 2001

The attack on the World Trade Center and the Pentagon . . . was an act of war.
—California Senator Diane Feinstein, September 12, 2001

"The Earth Countered," page 41

Any honest attempt to create conditions for democratic reforms in Iraq and for a resolution of its humanitarian crisis must include US willingness to engage in real dialogue with the Iraqi government. First and foremost, Iraq must be given the opportunity to show its face where it counts, at the Security Council. Iraq's Deputy Prime Minister Tariq Aziz has repeatedly offered dialogue on all issues. This should no longer be rebuffed . . . Those who argue that this would constitute a propaganda victory for Saddam Hussein should be reminded that the resolution of this major international conflict is a pre-condition for averting a deepening global crisis. They should also understand that this is not about saving political faces but about saving human lives . . . . The international community—including the United States—must accept a multipronged intervention as a first step towards solving the crises in the Middle East. Dialogue and negotiations, not military confrontation, should be the basis for this approach.
—Hans von Sponeck, February, 2002

"Classes in Citizenship," page 47

Most children die within three months of admittance. Without proper equipment and drugs, what's the use of your knowledge?

—Dr. Assad Essa, chief resident, Basra Pediatrics and Maternity Hospital; September, 2002

"The Beast in Baghdad," page 48

The war [on terror] will not be over until Saddam Hussein's days in power are over. Now is the time to take the war to the den of the beast, to Baghdad itself. Under serious attack Saddam Hussein's regime will collapse as quickly and easily as did Muhammad Omar's Taliban.

—Jonathan I. Katz, Washington University physics professor, from "Whoever Bombs Baghdad Gets My Vote," 2002

"Kathy Kelly," page 50

In hospitals across Iraq, I and many others have watched children dying in pain in front of their parents. I have held many of these children in my arms and tried to comfort their mothers.

—Kathy Kelly, three-time Nobel Peace Prize nominee and co-founder of Voices in the Wilderness, November 4, 2002

"Bert Sacks," page 51

Bert Sacks quit his job as an engineer to volunteer full-time with Voices in the Wilderness. Bringing medicine and building friendships, he led thirteen fact-finding delegations to Iraq during the era of sanctions and war. He persuaded members of the US Congress as well as journalists and photographers from major newspapers to participate in some of these delegations. In August 2002, he received a ten-thousand-dollar fine for illegal travel to Iraq and for bringing "toys and medicine" to Iraq. He responded by raising ten thousand dollars, using it to purchase medicine, and delivering the medicine to hospitals in Iraq.

"Fresh Air," page 54

Because of the sanctions in place against Iraq at this time, it was a violation of United States law for an American to contribute in any way to the Iraqi economy without "specific, prior authorization" from the United States Office of Foreign Asset Control. This included the most ordinary transactions, the kinds that occur at any shop or store.

"Anger," page 64

This is a school. The whole community needs it. But look at this building. Do your children go to school in a building like this?—broken windows and doors, no paint, holes in the walls, bad electrical wires, no heat, no air conditioning . . . How can we teach here? And no pencils, no books! Families won't send their children to school because it's not safe. We have to send them home to go to the bathroom. This is the gift your country gives us. This is the gift of sanctions! Take a good look. And you talk about peace and freedom . . . Iraq is a rich country, but you have made us poor . . . Look at us! We are teachers not criminals. So why are we being punished? Why is your country shaking its fists? Why is your country threatening us? We haven't attacked you. We haven't threatened you. Go home. Go! Go! Leave us alone. We can take care of ourselves.

—Nadia, Basra schoolteacher, September 27, 2002

"I Wish—Letter to Sattar," page 77

. . . comrade[s] . . . rest assured that our struggle on earth will continue . . . Our struggle will be everywhere.

—Pablo Neruda, *Canto General*, writing about a massacre of people rallying for workers' rights.

"Seeing Sattar Again," page 79

We've been invaded, not just by America, but now everyone who wants to fight America comes to Iraq to do it . . . Every day we think it will get better, but we only see it gets worse and worse. It's especially bad for children. All they see and hear about is war.

—Sattar Jabbar, May 9, 2005, Berkeley, California

"Dancing on Iraqi Graves, an Election Night Report," page 81
In Washington, supporters of President Bush danced and celebrated late into the night.

—Associated Press, November 3, 2004

They are fighting for the presidency of America but all I care about is what the winner will do for my country. I support whoever will pull the American troops out of Iraq.

—Mustafa Nouri, a Basra merchant, November 3, 2004

"Shock and Awe," page 82
The goal of Rapid Dominance will be to destroy or so confound the will to resist that an adversary will have no alternative except to accept our strategic aims and military objectives. To achieve this outcome, Rapid Dominance must control the operational environment and through that dominance, control what the adversary perceives, understands, and knows.

—Harlan K. Ullman and James P. Wade, *Shock and Awe, Achieving Rapid Dominance*

"New Strategy in This War without Borders," page 84
In November, shortly after razing Nazzal Emergency Hospital to the ground, United States forces entered Fallujah General Hospital, the city's only healthcare facility for trauma victims, detaining employees and patients alike. According to medics on the scene, water and electricity were "cut off," ambulances confiscated, and surgeons, without exception, kept out of the besieged city.

—Dahr Jamail, report to the World Tribunal on Iraq, June 27, 2005

"Experiments in Freedom," page 85
An Iraqi man and his wife have been shot dead in front of their five children by United States soldiers who fired on the car in which the family was traveling. The children survived but emerged from the car spattered with blood, screaming and traumatised. The soldiers tended to them and brought them to hospital.

—*Irish Times*, January 20, 2005

Today, America speaks anew to the peoples of the world: All who live in tyranny and hopelessness can know: The United States will not ignore your oppression, or excuse your oppressors. When you stand for your liberty, we will stand with you.

—George W. Bush, Inaugural Address, January 20, 2005

114

"Lines Written in Footprints on the Piazza Stones," page 86

About 10,000 Italians paid their respects Sunday to an intelligence agent [Nicola Calipari] killed by US troops in Iraq last week while driving with Giuliana Sgrena, a hostage he had helped free. The body of Calipari lay in state at a large marble memorial called the Vittoriano in central Rome. Mourners filed past a flag-draped coffin, and many praised the slain agent as a hero.

—*Washington Post*, March 6, 2005

The unprovoked attack killed Nicola Calipari . . . He had thrown himself on top of Ms. Sgrena to shield her and was killed by a bullet through his temple.

—*The Independent*, March 6, 2005

"This Much We Know," page 87

I wrote several poems in November 2004 while participating in a four-day vigil in Lawton, Oklahoma, outside Fort Sill where Camilo Mejia was imprisoned for refusing to return to fight in Iraq. We wanted to support Mejia because, having fought in Iraq, he spoke with authority about the moral character of the war. We also supported him because he embodies a turning away from violence that we believe our world so desperately needs. Lawton is colored by the presence of Fort Sill. Young soldiers are a common sight on its streets and in its eateries and stores, and merchants across town advertise specials for military personnel. Standing at busy intersections with three-foot glossy photos of Iraqi children and handing out leaflets to passersby, we stood out like aliens. That is, until the soldiers' wives and fiancés, pushing children, came to talk to us, and the suicide of a Fort Sill soldier grounded us more deeply in our convictions.

"Letter to Camilo Mejia," page 88

I have held a rifle to a man's face, a man on the ground and in front of his mother, children, and wife and not known why I did it. I have seen a soldier broken down inside because he killed a child . . . I admit that in Iraq there was the fear of being killed, but there was also the fear of killing innocent people, the fear of putting myself in a position where to survive means to kill; there was the fear of losing my soul in the process of saving my body . . . I was afraid of waking up one morning to realize

my humanity had abandoned me . . . By putting my weapon down, I chose to reassert
myself as a human being.

—Sergeant Camilo Mejia

"The Other Side," page 89

The wide grass greenbelt which runs down the center of Gore Boulevard in Lawton is the annual site of a holiday-season, light festival. Over one million lights illuminate six city blocks of unique Christmas displays. When we arrived in Lawton, several of the displays were under construction, including a regiment of nutcracker toy soldiers, brightly colored and arranged in neat rows facing the street. We stood here one day among the toy soldiers, holding our three-foot, glossy color photos of Iraqi children.

"Some Questions About Torture," page 93

The "Murderous Maniacs" was what they called us at our camp because they knew
if they got caught by us and got detained by us . . . then it would be hell to pay. They
would be just, you know, you couldn't even imagine. It was . . . like a game. You know,
how far could you make this guy go before he passes out or just collapses on you. From
stress positions to keeping them up . . . two days straight, whatever. Deprive them
of food, water, whatever . . . On their day off people would show up all the time.
Everyone in camp knew if you wanted to work out your frustration you show up at the
PUC [person under control] tent . . . As long as no PUCs came up dead it happened.
We heard rumors of PUCs dying so we were careful. We kept it to broken arms and legs
and shit. If a leg was broken you called the PA—the physician's assistant—and told
him the PUC got hurt when he was taken. He would get Motrin and maybe a sling,
but no cast or medical treatment . . . At the same time . . . it was wrong. There's a set of
standards. But you gotta understand, this was the norm. Everyone would just sweep it
under the rug.
—United States Army Sergeant "A" from a July / August, 2005, interview by
Human Rights Watch.

"In These Offices," page 94

Nancy Pelosi has called the war "intolerable," but she continues to vote to fund it.
She has chosen not to support other efforts to bring our troops home now . . . She has
declined to support Barbara's Lee's resolution against a permanent US presence in Iraq.
Instead, she has voted to allocate funds for permanent bases.

—Bay Area United for Peace and Justice website, September 26, 2005

"Comes a Cleansing War," Page 96

President Bush pleaded for Americans' patience Wednesday . . . hours after more than thirty American troops perished in a helicopter crash in western Iraq and insurgents killed five others in the deadliest day yet for US forces.

—Terence Hunt, AP White House Correspondent, January 26, 2005

In the long run, there is no justice without freedom. . . . Eventually, the call of freedom comes to every mind and every soul . . . Liberty will come to those who love it . . . And as hope kindles hope, millions more will find it. By our efforts, we have lit a fire as well—a fire in the minds of men. It warms those who feel its power . . . and one day this untamed fire of freedom will reach the darkest corners of our world . . . We go forward with complete confidence in the eventual triumph of freedom . . . because freedom is the permanent hope of mankind, the hunger in dark places, the longing of the soul.

—George W. Bush, inaugural address, January 20, 2005

"Anywhere USA," page 97

Shelby West is the daughter of Army Master Sgt. Robert H. West. She was eleven in May 2006 when her father died in combat in Iraq (see note below under "Burning Books").

"A Letter from Your Mother," page 98

Jason Henderson was a Humvee mechanic in the US Army for five years. He deployed to Iraq for six months in 2003 and re-deployed in October of 2004. According to his mother, Janna, he returned to the States for a visit in December, 2004, and complained of difficulty swallowing. After returning to Iraq, he was treated for acid reflux. But the problem persisted and worsened. In March, 2005, he was transferred to the US military hospital in Landstuhl, Germany, where he was diagnosed with advanced stage cancer, affecting his stomach, esophagus, liver, and pancreas. At his family's request, he was transferred to Walter Reed Army Medical Center in Virginia. Not long afterward, he transferred home. According to Janna, a doctor at Walter Reed told her the cancer must have been caused by "an exposure over there." Janna states the US military will give her no information about the cause of Jason's illness. She states the "whole seventh floor (oncology) of Walter

Reed is full of patients…all young…men and women…all soldiers." Jason Henderson died August 13, 2005 in Ukiah at UVMC.

"Burning Books," page 99

Thirty-seven-year old Master Sgt. Robert H. West, from Elyria, Ohio, died in Baghdad on May 14, 2006 during combat operations when an improvised explosive device detonated next to his Humvee. Robert was a member of the US Army, assigned to the 1st Battalion, 4th Brigade, 78th Division out of Fort Bragg, NC. At the time of his death, he had a wife, Jeannie, and an eleven-year-old daughter, Shelby.

"Cindy Sheehan," page 101

Cindy Sheehan became a prominent American anti-Iraq war activist after the death of her son Casey Sheehan during his service in Iraq. Sheehan gained national attention in early August 2005 when she traveled to President Bush's Prairie Chapel Ranch just outside Crawford, Texas, during his five-week vacation retreat there. Demanding a second meeting with the President and an explanation of the "noble cause" for which her son died, she created a peace camp called Camp Casey by pitching a tent by the side of the road and announced her intention to stay day and night for the full five weeks or until such a meeting is granted. She has also promised that, if she is not granted a second meeting, she will return to Crawford each time Bush visits there in the future.

—*Wikipedia* (http://en.wikipedia.org/wiki/Cindy_Sheehan)

"Where Silence Can Have Its Say," page 104

It had taken just one wrong turn for disaster to unfold. Less than a mile from the base it was heading to, the convoy turned left instead of right and lumbered down one of the most anti-American streets in Iraq . . . As the lorries desperately tried to reverse out, dozens of Sunni Arab insurgents wielding rocket launchers and automatic rifles emerged from their homes . . . The mob grew more frenzied as the gunmen dragged two Americans from the cab of their bullet-ridden lorry and forced them to kneel on the street. Killing one of the men with a rifle round fired into the back of his head, they

doused the other with petrol and set him alight. Barefoot children, yelping in delight,
piled straw on to the screaming man's body to stoke the flames.

—*The Telegraph,* October 22, 2005

Acknowledgment

When I began to send letters of inquiry to publishers, I had no idea that producing this book of poetry would involve such a collaborative effort. Many people helped shape the book you hold in your hands. My deepest thanks to

—Marcia Gagliardi, the publisher, who guided every step of the process, for having the vision and fortitude to produce this book

—Copy editor Mary-Ann Palmieri for multiple close readings and skilled editing

—Sherrie Smith-Ferri for a hundred things: creative intelligence and level-headedness that I tapped countless times, unflagging support, and the many hours she spent reading poems, ordering them, and forging a vision that transformed a loose collection of poetry into a viable manuscript with a coherent storyline

—Laura Ferri for commenting on individual poems and helping organize the book

—Theresa Whitehill of Colored Horse Studios for her friendship, advice, and beautiful cover design

—Activist photographers whose photos appear on the cover or in the text: Alan Pogue of Texas Center for Documentary Photography, Doug Johnson and Jim Harney of Posibilidad, and Ted Sexauer of Veterans for Peace

—Evan Johnson of Evan Johnson Photography for humor and companionship and for editing and upgrading my photographs which appear in the text of the book

—Ken McCormick of Visual Identity for coordinating the printing

—Kathy Kelly for her beautiful foreword

Many people have supported my activism and my writing. Several deserve special mention. Barbara Lubin, director of the Middle East Children's Alliance, Simon Harak, SJ, Mike and Gerry Gospe, Kevin Keckes, Penny Rosenwasser, Laurie Carla Hasbrook, Dave Sylvester, Susan Crane, Phil Berrigan, Ardeth Platte, Frank Cordaro, Daniel Sicken, Jeffrey

St. Clair, editor at CounterPunch, Danny Muller, Rudy Simons, Eileen Malone, Janice Farrell, Scott Blackburn, who designed my web page, Cindy Litman, Maggie Coulter, and Patricia Daugherty. I am grateful to numerous friends here in Mendocino County who organized or participated in events when I returned from trips to the Middle East and who have cheered the publication of this book.

Every writer owes a debt to other writers. I want to thank Daniel Berrigan for his writing and for his correspondence over the years.

Though it seems so long ago, I thank my friend Elaine Fleck for the gift of that first book of Daniel Berrigan's poems and John Hession, whose enthusiasm for language and writing inspired me at an age when anything seemed possible and whose friendship helped shape my artistic sensibilities.

Last, I thank the people I met in Iraq for their unstinting hospitality and for the remarkable giving of themselves which I have tried to render in the these poems. It is out of solidarity with them that this book takes flight.

Proceeds from this book will support Iraqi victims of war. For more information, go to www.battlefieldwithoutborders.org.

Poet David Smith-Ferri in Amman, Jordan, loading medicine, clothing, and medical journals for distribution in Iraq in July, 1999.

—photo by Kathy Kelly

About the Author

David Smith-Ferri has been active in opposing US military and economic warfare against the people of Iraq since he first traveled to Iraq with Voices in the Wilderness in 1999. He continues his activism today as a member of Voices for Creative Nonviolence (www.vcnv.org). His poetry and essays about Iraq have appeared in *CounterPunch, Z Magazine, Yes! Magazine, The Witness,* and *The Other Side Magazine.* None of this work would be possible without the friendship and support of many people, especially his partner Sherrie, their daughter Rachael, and his mother-in-law Sally. He lives in northern California where he can be reached by email at david@battlefieldwithoutborders.org or at the website www.battlefieldwithoutborders.org.